W9-BJE-039

JANE KALLIR

ARNOLD SCHOENBERG'S VIENNA

GALERIE ST. ETIENNE/RIZZOLI

Exhibition dates: November 13, 1984—January 5, 1985
Organized with the support of Lufthansa German Airlines

Galerie St. Etienne
24 West 57th Street
New York, New York 10019

Published in 1984 by Galerie St. Etienne and Rizzoli
International Publications, Inc., 712 Fifth Avenue, New York,
New York 10019

Copyright © 1984 by Galerie St. Etienne, New York.
All rights reserved. No part of this book may be
reproduced or utilized in any form or by any means,
electronic or mechanical, including photocopying, recording,
or by any information storage and retrieval system,
without permission in writing from Galerie St. Etienne,
24 West 57th Street, New York, New York 10019.

Arnold Schoenberg illustrations Copyright © 1984,
Belmont Music Publishers.

ISBN: 0-8478-05808
LC: 84-62358

Designed by Gary Cosimini
Printed by John D. Lucas Printing Company, Baltimore, Maryland

Photographs by Geoffrey Clements, Walter Dräyer,
Marianne Gurley, Florence Homolka, Donald Hull, Eric Politzer,
H.H. Stuckenschmidt and Alan Dean Walker.

Cover: Arnold Schoenberg. *Tears.* Oil on canvas. 11 1/2" x 9".
(Schoenberg 129). Collection Lawrence and Ronald Schoenberg and Nuria
Schoenberg Nono.

Frontispiece: Richard Gerstl. *Portrait of Arnold Schoenberg.*
Oil on canvas. 71 5/8" x 51 1/8". (Kallir C). Historisches
Museum der Stadt Wien.

CONTENTS

Plate 1. Arnold Schoenberg: *Green Self-Portrait*. **1910. Oil on wood. 13 ″ x 9 1/2″. (Schoenberg 4). Collection Lawrence and Ronald Schoenberg and Nuria Schoenberg Nono.**

INTRODUCTION

Arnold Schoenberg's Vienna was a city of transition and turmoil, a city of somnambulists whose dream was gradually turning into a nightmare. In the decades preceding World War I, the Austrian monarchy moved ever closer to extinction, while throughout its realm the arts and sciences flourished with unparalleled vigor. Beneath a seemingly calm surface, underlying portents of doom could be traced in the gradual emergence of raw expressionism from the florid aestheticism of the *fin de siècle* period. Contrary to what one might expect, this was not a period of decadence and despair, but rather a time of unprecedented progress in all fields of human endeavor—a last burst of energy that was, paradoxically, fueled by the scarcely perceived imminence of collapse.

Much has been written, especially in recent years, about this twilight era of the Habsburg Empire, what the Austrians themselves nostalgically refer to as *"der letzte Glanz der Kaiserzeit"* (the last sparkle of the Imperial Age). Since the publication of *Wittgenstein's Vienna*[1] in 1973, hardly a year has gone by without the appearance of one or more "Vienna" books. While one would not want to give the Wittgenstein study sole credit for what has become a near fad (it was certainly not the first volume of its kind, and many of the later works were already in preparation when it was published), it crystallized an increasingly popular tendency to unify the various disparate cultural contributions of *fin de siècle* Vienna and postulate therefrom some kind of general model for twentieth-century European cultural history. Previously, individual Austrians had been recognized for their individual contributions; Freud, Wittgenstein, and Schoenberg, to name just three, were widely acknowledged as pioneers in their respective fields. However, the linking up of the various cultural manifestations was a relatively new trend.

Whatever the cause of the recent interest in turn-of-the-century Viennese culture, one of the chief components of the current "Vienna boom" was surely the rediscovery of that city's contributions to the visual arts. The two world wars interrupted the international flow of art history and placed the German-speaking countries behind a cultural blockade. Austria, whose identity was subsumed by that of Germany after World War I, was doubly disadvantaged. However, in the 1960s a revisionist approach to the evaluation of international modernism—which heretofore had been dominated by the French example—led to the reappraisal of Austrian art. This, in turn, seemed to provide general cultural historians with the missing piece they were looking for; suddenly the parts were made whole, and isolated accomplishments were transformed into a national phenomenon.

The actual role played by the arts during the period in question is undeniable. More than just a convenient premise for latter-day historians, the arts really were an important ingredient in the glue that held Viennese society together. The *Wiener Werkstätte*, an Austrian variant of the British Arts and Crafts movement, attempted to aestheticize every aspect of human life. The small-town atmosphere of Vienna—alternately *gemütlich* or oppressive, depending on one's mood— ensured that artists would mingle, both socially and intellectually, with their colleagues in other fields. Thus the composer Gustav Mahler married Alma Schindler, daughter of the prominent painter Emil Jakob Schindler. Ludwig Wittgenstein's father helped finance the Secession, and his sister had her portrait painted by Gustav Klimt. The architect Adolf Loos picked out a young artist, Oskar Kokoschka, at the 1908 *Kunstschau* (Art Show) and transformed him into an object lesson demonstrating his own avant-garde aesthetic theories. Artistic causes became rallying cries for Vienna's intellectual community, and aesthetic issues occasioned far-reaching philosophical debates.

Of all the encounters that took place between the various branches of the arts in Vienna at the turn of the century, perhaps the most mysterious was that between the composer Arnold Schoenberg and a brash young painter named Richard Gerstl. Their relationship lasted scarcely three years, and when it ended, the twenty-five-year-old painter was dead. Before taking his life in 1908, Gerstl destroyed almost all documentary evidence of his existence, but he left behind a legacy of paintings that rank among the most advanced work of their time. Schoenberg may have dabbled in art before he met Gerstl, and he certainly painted a little during the period of their acquaintance. However, after Gerstl's suicide the composer attacked his canvases with an unprecedented fervor, and by 1910 he had enough for a small exhibition.

That Schoenberg's paintings surpassed the efforts of the average dilettante was confirmed in 1912, when Wassily Kandinsky chose to feature them prominently in the *Blaue Reiter* Almanac. Schoenberg's haunting "Visions" and "Gazes" inadvertently illustrated Kandinsky's theory that the untrained artist is, at times, able to attain an expressive purity that is beyond the reach of his academically educated colleagues. However, Schoenberg was hardly "naive" in the same sense as the French painter Henri Rousseau, with whom Kandinsky compared him. In feeling and in intent, the composer's paintings are clearly allied with those of the Austrian expressionists Oskar Kokoschka and Egon Schiele. Indeed, Schoenberg's emergence as a painter overlaps so completely with the first expressionist outpourings of his compatriots that his art must to some extent be considered as part of that general movement. It is no coincidence that his brief painting career, which (for all practical purposes) ended in 1912, occurred in tandem with the composer's "emancipation of dissonance," a breakthrough that musicologists (again as a matter of no small coincidence) commonly term "expressionistic."

The simultaneous advent of expressionism in Schoenberg's music, in his paintings, and in the paintings of his contemporaries is a reflection of forces that transcend the contributions of any one individual. Schoenberg, because of his great and multifaceted genius, became a catalyst for these forces. He himself often noted that he did what he did out

Figure 1. Richard Gerstl: *Self-Portrait*. **Ca. 1906. Pen and ink on buff wove paper. 17 3/4″ x 12 3/8″. (Kallir 60). Estate of Otto Kallir.**

Figure 2. *Arnold Schoenberg*. Ca. 1910. The Arnold Schoenberg Institute, University of Southern California, Los Angeles.

Figure 3. Arnold Schoenberg: *Self-Portrait*. Brush and ink on off-white wove paper, mounted on cardboard. 8 7/8″ x 5 3/4″. (Schoenberg 32). Collection Lawrence and Ronald Schoenberg and Nuria Schoenberg Nono.

of necessity, that he responded to an overriding power beyond his control. Yet in allowing himself to be shaped by the demands of his times, he himself gave shape to those times. It is in this sense that Schoenberg's paintings, no less than his music, may be seen as a key to the very essence of expressionism. As so often in early twentieth-century Viennese culture, it is the visual element that unites the different components and completes the jigsaw-puzzle picture.

The present book may be considered as a companion piece both to the existing musicological biographies of Schoenberg and to the existing studies on Viennese art. As such, it is neither an examination of Schoenberg's music nor of Austrian expressionism per se. Rather, like Schoenberg's paintings, it falls somewhere in between. While focusing on the paintings, which form the central chapter, this study recognizes that Schoenberg was not an artist in the usual sense, and that therefore an understanding of Schoenberg as composer, Schoenberg as man, and finally Schoenberg as product of his environment is crucial to the comprehension of Schoenberg as painter. Because the book centers around the paintings and, in particular, Schoenberg's period in Vienna, later events in his life are discussed only insofar as they relate to tendencies established earlier and are necessary to "finish the story." By the same token, many of Schoenberg's major musical compositions are passed over in order to concentrate on those that directly relate to his expressionist breakthrough.

This book could also have been titled *Arnold Schoenberg and Vienna*, for it is less a document of a particular time and place than of one man's interaction with that time and place. The existing literature has already adequately demonstrated how individual men, working simultaneously toward their individual goals, contributed to and created the collective entity that has been popularized under the euphemistic rubric *fin de siècle* Vienna. These studies take the long view, presenting surveys, from differing perspectives, of the macrocosm. The present book is a study of Vienna in microcosm as seen through the achievements of a single person, Arnold Schoenberg. We have, so to speak, turned the telescope around and are now looking from the broad horizon of the present into one pinpoint moment of the past, rather than vice versa, as has so often been the case.

Plotting social and artistic connections is one of the chief goals of an investigation of this kind. There are periods, during the first decade of this century, when it almost seems as though a well-connected Viennese sophisticate could have attended a groundbreaking cultural event every day. However, that does not necessarily mean that Schoenberg, who was always primarily concerned with his music, was aware of everything that was going on around him. Certain questions—When exactly did he begin to paint? Did Gerstl teach him? When did Schoenberg first meet Kokoschka? Were the composer's aesthetic theories influenced by those of Kandinsky?—assume primary importance, and some of them can never be satisfactorily answered. Moreover, even if one proves, as has now been conclusively done, that Schoenberg did not meet Kandinsky until 1911, but that he did, in fact—as was discovered in the course of preparing this book—know Kokoschka in 1909, what bearing does this have on Schoenberg's own artistic development?

Artistic allegiances can be deceptive. Given the basic hostility of the Viennese public to any sort of artistic innovation, one might expect artists to stick together. However, feelings could run high among the Viennese intelligentsia, and ideology was not everything. Thus Kokoschka could treat with disdain artists such as Schiele and Max Oppenheimer, with whom, on the basis of style, he should theoretically have been allied. On the other hand, Loos could welcome Klimt to his coffeehouse table after the opening of the *Kunstschau*, and then proceed to denounce everything Klimt stood for in a public lecture. Not only did one not always know who one's friends were, sometimes one did not even know whom to count among one's enemies. A certain degree of aesthetic paranoia became unavoidable.

Like all cities, Vienna provided not just an artistic environment, but also a social and political one. Unusual, however, were the close connections that were established between various fields of endeavor, bringing ordinarily disparate elements to bear on one another. The relationships that existed between artists and their colleagues, and between artists and their public, must be viewed as contributing factors in any investigation of the period, for the interaction that occurs between a personality of genius and its environment in some way determines whether that personality bears the fruit of its latent promise, or withers unfulfilled. Arnold Schoenberg's psychic makeup and responses are intrinsic to his work. The kind of music he wrote determined the circumstances of his life, and those circumstances shaped, in turn, his personality and his art. Thus a study of early twentieth-century Vienna should not be considered simply an exercise in nostalgia, or even merely a journey back to an interesting but remote time that produced a disproportionate number of great men. It is, rather, a study in the circumstances that define greatness.

Plate 2. Arnold Schoenberg: *Self-Portrait.* **1911. Oil on cardboard. 18 7/8" x 17 3/4". (Schoenberg 7). Collection Lawrence and Ronald Schoenberg and Nuria Schoenberg Nono.**

PRELUDE

Arnold Schoenberg[1] was born in Vienna in 1874, the son of a Jewish shopkeeper, Samuel, and his wife, Pauline. There is no solid evidence that either of Arnold's parents was particularly musical, although his father is said to have been a member of a choral society, and his mother came from a long line of cantors. At any rate, music was beyond the means of the Schoenbergs, who could afford neither concert tickets nor a piano, a standard domestic accouterment in these days before phonographs and radios. Young Arnold had to content himself with the violin, which he began studying at the age of eight. At ten he started composing; it is said that he created a new piece for each violin lesson. When he grew older, he would wander the paths of the Prater, Vienna's large public amusement park, listening to the music that emanated from the coffeehouses there. The price of a cup of coffee would have bought him a place inside, but even this was more than he could manage. To obtain unreserved seats at the opera—which were offered daily at a reduced price—Schoenberg and his friends stood in line from three o'clock until seven, when the doors opened, and then raced each other up the stairs to claim their bounty.

Given his family's financial circumstances, Schoenberg could not expect much encouragement for his musical inclinations. His father wanted him to be an engineer, but even this goal proved unrealistic. When Samuel Schoenberg succumbed to an influenza epidemic in 1890, the boy was forced to leave school. His mother got him an apprenticeship at a bank, but Arnold's true ambitions could not be so easily squelched. Much to the ire of his new employer, he covered all his official bank papers with musical notes. Nonetheless, the reluctant apprentice managed to keep his job until 1895, when either he or his boss, or possibly the bankruptcy of the firm, put an end to the experience.

While still employed at the bank, Arnold Schoenberg made his first tentative steps toward his ultimate profession. It was around this time that he met Alexander von Zemlinsky (Figure 4), a composer and conductor who was the leader of the amateur orchestra Polyhymnia. Zemlinsky was a rising young talent in local music circles, having graduated with distinction from the Vienna Conservatory and earned the praises of no less than Johannes Brahms. Schoenberg obtained a job directing a workers' chorus, and to some extent aided by Zemlinsky, he began to receive free-lance orchestration assignments. Though as Charles Rosen, one of the composer's biographers, has pointed out, Schoenberg's free-lance work required a good deal of technical proficiency, he was essentially self-taught. As a boy he had had to look up musical terms in his parents' encyclopedia. Now Zemlinsky, three years his senior, became his mentor and teacher. The lessons, however, were free-form at best, and Schoenberg always retained a healthy disdain for "book learning." "One only learns what one knows anyhow," he later said.[2]

Through Zemlinsky, a whole new world opened up to Schoenberg. The poor Jewish boy from the Second District ghetto crossed over the Danube Canal and entered the heart of the city. Over the course of the next five or six years, he logged in several hundred nights at the opera, and by the time he was twenty-five, he had seen each of Richard Wagner's operas close to thirty times. Zemlinsky not only introduced his protégé to Wagner's music, he also introduced him to the circle of young musicians that met regularly at the Cafe Griensteidl. "They were all rebels," Schoenberg's cousin Hans Nachod later remembered, "especially attractive to the younger generation…because they were unconventional in the conventional surroundings of old traditional Vienna."[3] Arnold took enthusiastic part in drunken revels that often lasted until dawn, entertaining his buddies with his pert but somewhat abrasive wit.

Much has been written about the institution of the Viennese coffeehouse, with its complimentary newspapers and obligatory little glasses of water. Home away from home (or, for victims of Vienna's chronic housing shortage, home itself), post office, and social club all rolled into one, the coffeehouse has gone down in history as the place where, in the late nineteenth century, vanguard intellectuals met to shape the future. In the 1890s the Café Griensteidl was Vienna's leading literary coffeehouse. Opened in 1847 on a square not far from the Burgtheater, it immediately became a natural meeting place for writers and actors. Over the course of the ensuing decades, the coffeehouse itself acquired a genteel shabbiness, its once white wallpaper yellowed with smoke, while its reputation developed a glowing patina. "Café Megalomania," the cynics dubbed it: the center of the literary movement known as *Junges Wien* (Young Vienna), whose members, including the poet Hugo von Hofmannsthal and the playwright Arthur Schnitzler, gathered regularly around the table of the critic Hermann Bahr.

The poet laureate of the coffeehouse scene was surely Peter Altenberg (Figure 44), the black sheep of a well-to-do family, who, having failed at every profession he had ever halfheartedly tried, now made a profession of hanging out. He emerged from obscurity on the periphery of the *Junges Wien* group when Schnitzler[4] discovered a series of essays, based on Altenberg's coffeehouse experiences, that were eventually published under the title *Lokalen Chronik* (*Pub House Chronicles*). By 1896, Altenberg had abandoned the Griensteidl for the roomier and less crowded Café Central down the street. Here the thirty-seven-year-old eccentric became something of a mascot to a group that called itself the "triumvirate of betters," and whose other two members were Adolf Loos (Figure 44) and Karl Kraus. Loos, who would one day be hailed among the modern era's most innovative architects, was then twenty-six years old and had just returned from an extended visit to the United States. Kraus, a philosophy student four years Loos's junior, had already made a name for himself as a journalist and would later found the legendary satirical

Figure 4. Richard Gerstl: *Portrait of Alexander von Zemlinsky*. **Oil on canvas. 67" x 29 1/8". (Kallir 40). Private collection.**

Figure 5. *Alban Berg with Schoenberg's portrait of him*. **Ca. 1932. The Arnold Schoenberg Institute, University of Southern California, Los Angeles.**

periodical *Die Fackel* (The Torch). Kraus, who like Altenberg had once sat at Bahr's table, grew to despise the entire *Junges Wien* movement, and when, toward the end of 1896, the Griensteidl was demolished, he published a notorious attack under the title "The Demolished Literature."

In the course of the ensuing decades, the iconoclasts at Loos's table would draw into their orbit kindred spirits in the various arts, sweeping aside the last remnants of bourgeois convention and the pallid aestheticism of Bahr's contingent. One may fantasize about conversations overheard or shared in those early days at the Griensteidl, where Loos still sometimes sat — glaring, one might presume, at the offensive Bahr. Schoenberg later befriended both men, though there is no evidence that he met either of them at the Griensteidl. They were simply latent presences in his widening social orbit. One person whom he *did* meet at this time, however, was the beautiful Alma Schindler, future bride of Gustav Mahler. Then a pupil of Zemlinsky, she would eventually become one of Schoenberg's staunchest friends and supporters.

Alma Schindler's background was as different from Schoenberg's as day from night. The Schindlers moved in the most rarified art circles. As a baby, Alma had been bedded in a cradle given her by Hans Makart, court painter to the Emperor Franz Josef, and the most successful artist of his day. Emil Jakob Schindler, Alma's father, was a well-known landscapist, and even if money was sometimes scarce in his household, luxury items were not. After Schindler's death, Alma's mother married the painter Carl Moll. As Moll turned increasingly to art dealing, the family's fortunes improved, and by 1901 they were able to afford a mansion on Vienna's elegant Hohe Warte. Alma's indefinable allure — as much the product of intelligence and talent as of good looks — made her the talk of Vienna. While still a teen-ager, she was pursued by the thirty-five-year-old painter Gustav Klimt, Makart's protégé and, following the elder painter's death in 1884, his heir apparent. Schoenberg's first meeting with this budding femme fatale at Zemlinsky's house was hardly auspicious. Alma was dismayed by the young composer's shabby clothing, and recoiled in disgust. Zemlinsky gently admonished her, "Have a good look...the world will have a lot to say about him."[5]

Schoenberg was undoubtedly as immune to Alma Schindler's charms as she to his, for the intense young composer was almost wholly absorbed by his struggle to acquire the technical knowledge needed to give form to his inner vision. As the new century dawned, he turned away from Brahms, whose example he had been following, and toward Wagner, whose notion of a *Gesamtkunstwerk* (total artwork) — a unification of all the arts in a single operatic piece — had by now become familiar to him. Intrigued by this concept, he looked to literary works for inspiration. He was particularly susceptible to the poems of Richard Dehmel, which seemed to mirror his burgeoning passion for Zemlinsky's sister Mathilde (Figure 7). Schoenberg spent the summer of 1899 with the two siblings in the Austrian countryside, and here, in November, he wrote his first great composition, *Verklärte Nacht* (Transfigured Night), based on a Dehmel homage to ideal love.

Arnold and Mathilde were married in October 1901. As their first child, Gertrud, was born just four months after the wedding, it may be assumed that a necessity more powerful than Dehmel's perfect love had entered the relationship. Schoenberg was begin-

**Figure 6. Arnold
Schoenberg:** *Portrait*.
**Pastel on cream wove
paper. 15 3/4" x 11 7/8".
(Schoenberg 94).
Collection Lawrence
and Ronald
Schoenberg and Nuria
Schoenberg Nono.**

**Figure 7. Arnold
Schoenberg:** *Portrait
of Mathilde
Schoenberg*. **Oil on
cardboard. 14 1/8" x
9 7/8". (Schoenberg 80).
Collection Lawrence
and Ronald
Schoenberg and Nuria
Schoenberg Nono.**

ning to achieve some limited success as a composer, but he was hardly in a position to support a wife and child. Shortly before his wedding he auditioned a few of his songs for the proprietor of the *Überbrettl*, a Berlin-based cabaret that was in Vienna on tour. In November of that year the *Überbrettl* moved into permanent quarters in Berlin, and soon thereafter Schoenberg signed on as conductor and staff composer. The salary was modest, but at least it provided the family with a steady income. Arnold packed up his pregnant wife, and by the end of 1901 they were settled in Berlin.

Schoenberg's association with the *Überbrettl* lasted a scant six months, for the financial failure of the enterprise precluded the renewal of his contract. However, during the year and a half that he spent in Berlin, the pattern of his future life began to take shape. The defining circumstance was poverty. To make ends meet, Schoenberg was forced to copy or orchestrate the work of other composers, or, later, to teach—activities that robbed him of the ability to pursue his own work full-time. His compositions were received poorly if, indeed, they were even performed at all. Counterbalancing these negative factors was the moral and financial support offered by a select group of colleagues.

In Berlin, Schoenberg's most important champion was fellow composer Richard Strauss. Strauss helped him obtain copy work and tried to arrange for him to teach at the Stern Conservatory. When these efforts proved inadequate, he offered him a personal loan and managed to secure him a grant from the Liszt Foundation. Nonetheless, it seemed to Schoenberg that he might be better off in Vienna, where he had more professional contacts, and so, in the summer of 1903, he decided to return.

Schoenberg found an apartment in the same building as his brother-in-law, Zemlinsky. The younger composer's mentor once again did his utmost to help him. Zemlinsky convinced Universal Edition, a newly founded music publisher, to give him copying assignments and recommended him for a teaching position at the Schwarzwald School. Despite this, and despite the Liszt Foundation grant, which was renewed in 1904, Schoenberg was still forced to appeal to a charity for assistance. Recognizing that teaching was the most agreeable source of income open to him, he endeavored to assemble a circle of private students, among the first of whom was a young doctoral candidate at the University of Vienna named Anton Webern. Dr. Guido Adler, a professor at the university, apparently referred people to him, and Schoenberg tried to solicit additional pupils with a newspaper advertisement. It was through the latter method that, in the autumn of 1904, he obtained another important student, Alban Berg (Figure 5). Webern and Berg, probably the most famous of the composer's disciples, would also become two of his closest friends.

His financial troubles notwithstanding, Schoenberg was quickly becoming integrated into the cultural fabric of Vienna. The seeds that had been planted before he left for Berlin now blossomed into full-fledged relationships. The Schwarzwald School, a progressive institution run by the wife of a wealthy banker, attracted many leading figures from the Viennese avant- garde. Loos taught there, and for a brief period much later, so did the painter Oskar Kokoschka. Apparently it was here, in 1904 or 1905, that Loos and Schoenberg first met. It was also around this time that Schoenberg entered the circle of the controversial director of the Vienna Opera, Gustav Mahler (Figure 8). Mahler's brother-in-law, Arnold Rosé, was the leader of a string quartet that bore his name and that had, in 1902, given the first performance of *Verklärte Nacht*. Shortly after Schoenberg returned to Vienna from Berlin, Rosé introduced him to Mahler, and soon he and Zemlinsky were welcomed as guests in Mahler's home.

At first, Schoenberg was put off by Mahler's superior manner, and Mahler by the cocky upstart's arrogance. A full-scale argument erupted, and Schoenberg, banned from the Mahler household, swore he would never return even if he *were* invited. Tempers cooled, however, and before long Zemlinsky and Schoenberg were accepted as regular members of Mahler's circle. As his appreciation of Mahler deepened, Schoenberg sorely regretted his abrasive behavior. "It was like a young girl," he apologized, "love that pursues with hate."[6] The young composer's passionate absorption in his own creative vision sometimes caused him to inadvertently trample the toes of those who, by virtue of age or renown, should have been judged his betters. Nevertheless, he could also be cowed into an agony of humility before someone he admired. Greeting Strauss after a concert, he recalled, "I was embarrassed like a fifteen-year-old boy, I stammered and certainly made . . . the impression of an unappealing servility.'"[7] He had a profound respect

Figure 8. Arnold Schoenberg: *Gustav Mahler*. **1910. Oil on cardboard. 17 3/4" x 16 7/8". (Schoenberg 76).**
Collection Lawrence and Ronald Schoenberg and Nuria Schoenberg Nono.

for the genius of men like Strauss and Mahler, and the support that they gave him moved him almost beyond words.

The extreme hostility of the Viennese public toward any sort of new music made the encouragement of one's comrades increasingly important. Whereas innovations in the visual arts were sustained by the backing of a small but wealthy group of bourgeois sophisticates, there was no such support structure for avant-garde musicians. Vienna's musical past was legendary, and the city's inhabitants, who could claim such luminaries as Mozart, Haydn, Beethoven, and Brahms in their collective ancestry, were almost all, regardless of social or economic class, self-appointed music experts. This overwhelming interest in things musical was equaled only by the extreme conservatism of the public's tastes, and the combination proved inimical to any composer who dared challenge the status quo. Hissing or whistling through the hollow ends of their door keys was the way concertgoers routinely expressed their disapproval of the unfamiliar. Although Schoenberg's first public performance, in 1897, had been received favorably, his second was not. As the composer later observed, from that time on "the scandal . . . never ceased."[8] One wag commented on *Verklärte Nacht* that it sounded "as if someone had smeared the score of *Tristan* while it was still wet."[9] During the 1905 premiere of his tone poem *Pelleas und Melisande*, the audience did not stop with mere hissing, but actually walked out en masse in the middle of the performance, making a point of loudly banging the doors.

The rudeness of the Viennese public was matched only by that of the Viennese press. The quality of the writing was sometimes so abysmal that today Austrians still use the adjective "journalistic" as a derogatory term. Every detail of a performance underwent minute scrutiny; even the way Mahler waved his baton was subject to ridicule. During his tenure at the Vienna Opera, the press pursued him mercilessly, transforming every small internal squabble into a full-blown scandal. The leading critic of the period, Eduard Hanslick, led the attacks against Mahler's compositions, which occasioned criticism even more brutal than his activities at the Opera. Of Mahler's *Second Symphony*, Hanslick wrote, "One of us must be mad, and it isn't I."[10]

As the twentieth century progressed, and the number of modernist innovations multiplied not only in music but in other fields as well, the intensity of the critical onslaught increased. Attack and defend became standard operating procedure. Artists grew accustomed to living with a siege mentality and banded together for protection against the Philistine hordes. The establishment of formal associations— performance groups such as the Ansorge *Verein* or exhibition halls such as the Secession—was a natural outgrowth of coffeehouse conviviality.[11] Schoenberg was not immune to the Viennese penchant for organizing—in 1904, he persuaded Mahler to assume the honorary presidency of an "Association of Creative Artists"—though he probably derived more satisfaction from the companionship of his own students and friends. The willingness of protégés like Webern and Berg to take up and even surpass the most advanced aspects of Schoenberg's own methodology graphically confirmed the validity of his vision.

Artistic alliances based on the recognition of an underlying aesthetic affinity could often be interdisciplinary. Loos, playing a triple role as architect, critical writer, and patron, was particularly vociferous in promoting the careers of those he judged his spiritual colleagues. Although notoriously hard of hearing, he became one of Schoenberg's most adamant defenders simply on principle. The composer was not unaware of the irony of this circumstance and later voiced mild disapproval: "It almost seems as though for Loos I am merely a modernist opportunity."[12] Nevertheless, Loos was willing to put his money where his mouth (if not his ear) was, as when he single-handedly financed a Schoenberg concert.[13] He described a typical incident as follows:

> By midday, not a single ticket had been sold. On the spur of the moment, I gathered up the last of my money and bought out the entire house. Then I stood on the Kärntnerstrasse and handed out tickets—to acquaintances and strangers, whoever came along. That night it was packed. We friends distributed ourselves throughout the hall, in order to intercede in the event of a riot.[14]

One wonders whether Loos's cavalier generosity in distributing the tickets may have produced a less than enthusiastic audience, though in any case it is clear that he planned his strategy down to the last detail.

With the marriage of Gustav Mahler to Alma Schindler in 1902, Viennese music and art were wed. Carl Moll, Alma's stepfather, was a founding member of the Secession, and it was probably he who convinced Mahler to prepare an arrangement of Beethoven's *Choral Symphony* for the opening of the Secession's special Beethoven exhibition. From this relationship, too, derived Mahler's collaboration with Alfred Roller, an artist who although lacking prior theatrical experience, became one of the most imaginative stage designers the Vienna Opera had ever known. In the Mahler household, painters, sculptors, and architects mingled freely with the composer's musical friends. It was here, perhaps, that Schoenberg, previously remote from artistic developments, had his first encounters with painters. Alban Berg, a devotee of coffeehouse society, strengthened the connection when in 1905 he joined Kraus, Loos, Klimt, and the painter Max Oppenheimer (known as Mopp) at Peter Altenberg's *Stammtisch* (regular table) in the Münchener-Löwenbräu Restaurant.[15]

At around this time, a totally unknown young painter approached, from a distance, the august circle that surrounded Gustav Mahler. He encountered Mahler in front of the parliament building and asked if he might paint his portrait. Mahler refused. Whether the two ever got any closer than this is not known.[16] The painter, Richard Gerstl (Figure 10), admired Mahler immensely, but it is likely that he found Arnold Schoenberg more accessible. One evening at a Mahler concert, he introduced himself to Schoenberg and Zemlinsky.

Later, Schoenberg would refer to Gerstl as "this person [who] invaded my house,"[17] but there is little doubt that at the time he welcomed the painter warmly. Schoenberg was glad to share his ideas with anyone interested enough to listen, and Gerstl, from all indications, was a very eager listener indeed. Ill at ease with his fellow painters (even his closest friend, the artist Victor Hammer [Figure 9], was rarely allowed to see his work and never to address him with the familiar "du"), he was drawn to the world of music and even toyed with the idea of becoming a music critic. Apparently he made his first

Figure 9. *Victor Hammer and Richard Gerstl*. Collection Carolyn Hammer.

Figure 10. William Clarke Rice: *Portrait of Richard Gerstl*. 1907. Oil on canvas. 26" x 20 1/2". Private collection.

advances to the Schoenberg group as early as 1905, and by 1907 he was such an integral member that he accompanied the family to the summer resort of Gmunden, staying next door to Webern.[18] The oft-repeated contention that Gerstl moved into the same Vienna apartment house as Schoenberg has not been substantiated, though it is certain that they both lived on the Liechtensteinstrasse.[19] In any case, they were close enough. Too close, as it turned out, for comfort.

Gerstl was a temperamental young man, and it is difficult to determine whether his belligerence stemmed from deeply felt aesthetic convictions or deep-seated emotional problems. Probably both factors were at work. Gerstl had no tolerance of the opinions of those he considered his intellectual inferiors. An amateur painter who gave well-intentioned advice was shown to the door; another visitor's praise caused Gerstl to slash the painting in question, so despicable did he find his admirer's taste. Once, while he was copying a picture at the Kunsthistorisches Museum, the director happened by and made a comment. "Don't disturb me," Gerstl snarled. "What do you know anyway?"[20] Unable to accept discipline or authority of any kind (or, at least, of a kind he deemed arbitrary), he had, as a boy, flitted from one school to another. At the Vienna Academy of Fine Arts, he was unfortunate enough to land in the class of one of the most reactionary professors, Christian Griepenkerl, and after several years[21] of intermittent sparring with his master, the boy was not accepted back for the final term. Through his friend Victor Hammer, he was instead taken into the class of Heinrich Lefler, a painter of more liberal persuasion.

Gerstl's association with the renegade Schoenberg faction certainly did nothing to assuage his habitual feelings of outrage. By 1907 the gap between Schoenberg's supporters and detractors had grown so wide that the two opposing sides were rather like armed camps prepared to fight it out on the battleground of the concert hall. The composer's development was leading him inexorably toward a break with the tonal system that had been the foundation of Western music since the Renaissance, and the results provoked increasing agitation whenever his work was performed. At a February 1907 concert, the audience, after leveling a resounding barrage of hissing at the compositions, left via the emergency exit. Mahler retaliated by applauding loudly, and challenged one of the hissing protestors. "I hiss at your *Dreck* symphonies, too," the man retorted.[22] In private, however, Mahler confessed to his wife, "I don't understand his music, but he is young; perhaps he is right. I am old and perhaps do not have the ear for his music anymore."[23] Supporting the avant-garde now required a leap of faith.

By the end of 1907, Schoenberg must have felt himself to be almost entirely alone. His most esteemed ally, Mahler, physically and emotionally exhausted by his ordeal at the Vienna Opera, tendered his resignation in the summer of that year to accept a post as director of New York's Metropolitan Opera. On December 9 a group of about two hundred admirers, invited by Webern, the critic Paul Stefan, and two of their friends, met at the train station to see the Mahlers off. The crowd, which had filled the railway carriage with flowers, included Klimt, Roller, Gerstl, and, naturally, the entire Schoenberg group. A reporter approached Gerstl, asking for a few words about the event. "I am not here to get my name in the papers," the painter snapped. "I am here for Gustav Mahler."[24] As the train pulled out of the station, Klimt muttered, *"vorbei"*—finished.

Gerstl, as a member of Schoenberg's entourage, became doubly isolated; as a painter, he was separated from other painters, and even as a music aficionado, he was separated from the ranks of other musicians. His sense of disorientation was exacerbated by Loos's diatribes against the prevailing tendency to merge the fine and the applied arts. While it was all well and good to say what art should *not* be, Loos could offer no concrete alternatives to the existing order. As a result, Gerstl became more and more antagonistic toward anything associated with the artistic "establishment," even when it meant damaging his own career. An exhibition at the progressive Galerie Miethke, possibly arranged through Schoenberg's connections with Carl Moll, had to be canceled when Gerstl refused to have his work hung together with that of Klimt, who was to be included in the show. When he heard that Lefler was participating in preparations for a *Festzug* (Festival Parade) honoring the Emperor Franz Josef on the sixtieth anniversary of his reign, the two quarreled, and Gerstl was asked to vacate his teacher's studio. The indignant student must have denounced the *Festzug*, which was enthusiastically supported by the *Wiener Werkstätte* crafts collective, as typical of that organization's tendency to waste genuine talent on evanescent spectacle.

Figure 11. *Mathilde Schoenberg*. Ca. 1911-15. The Arnold Schoenberg Institute, University of Southern California, Los Angeles.

Figure 12. Richard Gerstl: *Portrait of Mrs. Arnold Schoenberg*. Oil on canvas. 37 1/8" x 29 3/8". (Kallir 37). Österreichische Galerie, Vienna.

Gerstl's own artistic development had led him further and further beyond the limits of acceptable image making. Lefler, before their disagreement, considered mounting an exhibition and despaired. There was no safe way to show the paintings without provoking a scandal of major proportions. The Ansorge *Verein* was willing to take the risk, but Gerstl vetoed the exhibition for no apparent reason. He was becoming increasingly alienated and disturbed. A once meticulous dresser, he now ceased to look after himself. Had the artist been less introverted and reclusive, perhaps someone might have noticed that he was on the brink of disaster.

Love, under such circumstances, can be a man's salvation, but it can also be a final desperate attempt to make contact before plunging into the void. Of all the members of the Schoenberg circle, Gerstl found himself inexplicably attracted to the composer's wife (Figures 11, 12 and 13), a cipher of a woman who seemed, more often than not, simply to fade into the background. Mathilde Schoenberg was frail of health and did not mingle much with her husband's friends. There are indications that the marriage was never a strong one. It had been strained by a difficult pregnancy and the birth in 1906 of a second child, Georg. By 1907 the marriage was on the verge of collapse.

Figure 13. Richard Gerstl: *Mother and Child (Mathilde and Gertrud Schoenberg).* **Oil on canvas. 62 1/4″ x 46″. (Kallir D). Österreichische Galerie, Vienna.**

How long the affair went undetected is unknown. Certainly Arnold Schoenberg had no suspicions when, in the summer of 1908, he again invited Gerstl to join the family on holiday in Gmunden. But then, like many a cuckold, he did not want to recognize the situation that was unfolding subtly before his eyes:

> I denied the fact that my wife betrayed me . . . . She lied—I believed her. If I had not believed her, would she have remained with me so long? Wrong! She did not lie to me. For my wife does not lie. The soul of my wife is so united with my own that I know everything about her. Consequently, she did not lie; or else she was not my wife. And so it is. The soul of my wife was so alien from mine that I could not arrive at either a truthful or a dishonest relationship with her. We never really spoke with one another—i.e., communicated—we just talked...We never knew each other. I also do not even know what she looks like. I cannot conjure up her likeness. Perhaps she does not exist at all. She lives only in my imagination.[25]

Mathilde, caught in flagrante by Arnold in their Gmunden hideaway, was triumphantly whisked back to Vienna by her lover.[26] Schoenberg, in despair, wrote out a will that in parts reads like a suicide note. He seriously contemplated taking his life. The double betrayal of his wife and a man whom he had surely considered his friend must have been particularly painful in the light of his professional imbroglios. He had come to expect regular attacks from the Vienna press and public but had hoped that his inner circle was inviolable. For the moment, it must suddenly have seemed that there was no one on whom he could depend.

Fortunately, Webern came to the rescue, appealing to Mathilde's sense of motherhood and convincing her to return, if not for Arnold's sake, then for the sake of their two young children. On November 5, 1908, not long after the couple's reconciliation, Gerstl was found dead in his studio. The night before, the twenty-five-year-old painter had, with methodical precision, first burned all personal evidence of his existence, including a substantial portion of his oeuvre, then thrown a noose around his neck and, finally, plunged a knife into his chest. It does not require much imagination to envision the effect this event had on Mathilde. Years later, she still held a grudge against Webern for his role in the affair. For Schoenberg, too, the episode left scars that never completely healed, and even as an old man, he could be stung by a casual mention of Gerstl.[27] It was a situation that by its very nature was destined to prove disastrous to all concerned.

The close temporal relationship between Schoenberg's final break with conventional tonality and the Gerstl affair is, in the eyes of many of the composer's biographers, no coincidence. Schoenberg had, of course, come so far in his work that the next step was almost unavoidable. However, he feared taking it, and it is possible that the rupture of his marriage, in a strange way, gave him the necessary courage. "What difference, after all, does it make now?" he might have asked himself. In the summer of 1908 he completed his *Second String Quartet*, a work that in its last two movements reaches the very limits of tonality. He dedicated it, ironically, to his wife.

Much has been written about the quotation, in the second movement of the string quartet, of the folk song *Ach, du lieber Augustin*, whose lyrics include the line *"Alles ist hin"* (All is lost). The passage may be taken as referring either to the composer's marriage or, more figuratively, to his impending break with tonal tradition. Many years later, Schoenberg told one of his American students that the quotation was intended literally.[28] He may also have been making a deliberate allusion to Mahler's characteristic use of irony, which was apparently inspired by the same song. For Mahler, high tragedy became inextricably linked with frivolous entertainment when, as a child fleeing a parental argument, he came upon a hurdy-gurdy man cranking out the lilting strains of *Ach, du lieber Augustin*. The potency of this paradoxical juxtaposition is increased by the historical origins of the song itself, which like the English *Ring Around the Rosy*, is a cheerful homage to the Great Plague.[29] The sublimation of despair through laughter—a classic Viennese defense—or, as the case may be, the transformation of tragedy into art, was Schoenberg's solution to the dilemma posed by the Gerstl affair.

The first performance of the *Second String Quartet*, in December 1908, culminated in a near riot. As one observer described it:

> Part of the audience first giggled, then laughed and became restless; some shouted to the performers to stop . . . . Marie Gutheil-Schoder, the soprano, stood on the podium exposed to the fury of the scene and went on singing in tears. Afterward the noisemakers demanded that the hall be aired out so that the walls would be worthy of receiving Beethoven's *Harp Quartet*, which was next on the program.[30]

Regardless of the public's reaction (which was, by this time, predictable), Schoenberg had gone beyond the point of no return. Since March of 1908 he had worked intermittently on music to accompany Stefan George's poetic cycle *Das Buch der hängenden Gärten* (The Book of the Hanging Gardens), and this project provided the decisive opportunity. By September, the composer had eradicated all traces of structural harmony and, in the process, emancipated dissonance from its previous dependence on consonant resolution. "With the George songs," he explained, "I have for the first time succeeded in approaching an ideal of expression and form which has been on my mind for years. Until now, I lacked the strength and confidence to make it a reality . . . . I am being forced in this direction . . . . I am obeying an inner compulsion that is stronger than any upbringing."[31] "Atonality" was the name critics later gave to Schoenberg's innovation, a term which, in part because of its pejorative implications, the composer himself rejected. Alternatively, some use the adjective "expressionistic" to describe Schoenberg's work and that of his students from this period. The latter term, though in some ways as misleading as "atonality," reflects the composers' attempts to find musical correlatives for human emotional experiences, and also the convergence of this musical development with the advent of expressionism in the visual arts.

The difficulty of imposing order on a system that was by definition structureless, prompted Schoenberg, Webern, and Berg to write a number of exceedingly short pieces. As an alternative to this rather restrictive format, Schoenberg endeavored to give form to longer works by unifying them with a dramatic text. Between 1908 and 1913 he composed two musical dramas, *Erwartung* (Expectation) and *Die glückliche Hand* (The

Lucky Hand),[32] which attemped to combine text, music, and staging in a heretofore unprecedented manner. Because of certain similarities between these works and those of the Russian-born artist Wassily Kandinsky (most notably his 1909 stage piece *Der gelbe Klang* [The Yellow Sound]), many have sought to prove the existence of a mutual influence. However, as it is now clear that the two men did not meet until 1911, it must be accepted that they worked independently of one another. Kandinsky was developing an expressionist variant of the *Gesamtkunstwerk*, which was intended to surpass the Wagnerian prototype by treating each element individually rather than subordinating one to another. If the components of an operatic work—song, dance, music, staging, etc.—could be freed from their dependence on a superficial structure, they would each, like the individual notes of Schoenberg's "atonal" compositions, acquire greater expressive force. External disunity, Kandinsky believed, would make possible true internal unity.

Schoenberg's conception of *Erwartung* and *Die glückliche Hand* grew out of his already well-established belief that a musical composition must match the mood of the accompanying text but not necessarily its specific content—ideas that somewhat resemble those of Kandinsky. As he explained, he was not trying to achieve a literal interpretation of his chosen text:

> I have written many of my songs simply under the intoxicating influence of the tone of the opening words, without paying the least bit of attention to the further content of the poem, or understanding it at all. Carried away by the ecstasy of composing, I realized only days later what the content of my song was. At which point, to my surprise, it became evident that I could not possibly have been more faithful to the poet than I was when, led by the first unmistakable contact with the initial tone, I guessed what, of necessity, must obviously follow.[33]

Thus, like Kandinsky, Schoenberg achieved an internal unity of spirit without worrying about externally uniting music and text.

Whereas previously Schoenberg had relied on preexisting texts, he now sought texts custom-made to suit his purposes. *Erwartung* was commissioned from another writer, and *Die glückliche Hand* was written by the composer himself. The deliberate introduction of a dramatic element to his work, with its attendant requirements of actors, costumes, and staging, posed a new challenge requiring, to some extent, the collaboration of outside professionals. Schoenberg was not influenced by Kandinsky, but it now seems more than likely that he was at least cognizant of the dramatic innovations pioneered by the young Oskar Kokoschka.

By most accounts, the first expressionist drama ever performed was Oskar Kokoschka's *Mörder, Hoffnung der Frauen* (Murderer, Hope of Women), which was presented in July 1909. The play proposes a brutally extreme solution—murder—to the age-old battle of the sexes, here enacted by the prototypical characters "Man" and "Woman." Largely as a result of budgetary limitations, the actors' costumes were composed primarily of graphic body paint applied by the artist-playwright himself. The close correspondence between the visual appearance of the players and their written roles, and the presentation of a theme in terms of depersonalized allegorical figures, bears a marked similarity to Schoenberg's two dramas, particularly *Die glückliche Hand*. We do

Figure 14. Gustav Klimt: *Expectation*. Ca. 1905-09. Tempera, watercolor, gold, silver, and mixed media on paper. 76 1/8″ x 45 1/4″. Study for the Stoclet Frieze. (Novotny/Dobai 152B). Österreichisches Museum für angewandte Kunst, Vienna.

Figure 15. Gustav Klimt: *Fulfillment*. Ca. 1905-09. Tempera, watercolor, gold, silver, and mixed media on paper. 76 1/2″ x 47 3/8″. Study for the Stoclet Frieze. (Novotny/Dobai 152I). Österreichisches Museum für angewandte Kunst, Vienna.

not know whether the composer saw *Mörder*, though it is more than conceivable. Loos, who was by this time an ardent Kokoschka fan, specialized in routinely rounding up his friends whenever he felt one of his protégés needed an audience. Just as he later encouraged Kokoschka to attend Schoenberg's concerts, he may have invited the composer to contribute to the modernist "cause" by seeing the play. More conclusive than idle speculation, however, is a previously unrecorded series of letters that reveal that Schoenberg first contacted Kokoschka in the summer of 1909 with the apparent purpose of collaborating on a theatrical project. Contrary to what one might expect, it was not Loos who made the connection, but rather the painter Mopp, a colleague of Kokoschka's whom Schoenberg probably knew through Berg.[34] According to the correspondence, the composer actually met Kokoschka in the autumn of 1909.[35] The exact nature of Schoenberg's project remains unclear, though it is likely, judging from Kokoschka's scrawled advice ("the man should be halfway between softness and brutality"[36]), that it concerned the text for *Die glückliche Hand*, which the composer had begun in October 1908. This hypothesis is supported by the fact that Kokoschka was Schoenberg's first choice to create the set designs for *Glückliche Hand*. The composer had trouble with the development of this work and did not actually complete it until 1913. He may well have felt, in the summer of 1909, that he needed some help. It was also at this time that he commissioned the text for his monodrama *Erwartung*, and it could be that he at first wanted Kokoschka to contribute to this. Kokoschka did not respond immediately to Schoenberg's summons, and the assignment went to Marie Pappenheim, a young medical student whom Schoenberg met in the resort town of Steinachkirchen. Pappenheim had had her poetry published in *Die Fackel*, and this, to Schoenberg, was qualification enough.

Erwartung as a concept embodying the breathless anticipation of early love was a not uncommon theme in the arts at the turn of the century. Schoenberg had, in 1899, expressed his nascent love for Mathilde in a piece of this title. According to the traditional model, "expectation" is to be rewarded with "fulfillment," and it was thus that Klimt presented the two ideals in his Stoclet frieze (Figures 14 and 15). Schoenberg's 1909 *Erwartung*, on the other hand, was an upending, bordering on parody, of the standard treatment of the subject. The plot is brutally simple: A woman, lost in the woods, searches for her lover; at the end of the piece, she finds his corpse.

Given the similarities between this plot and the Gerstl affair, there has been a tendency to see the former as a direct reflection of the latter.[37] However, since Schoenberg did not write the text, such theorizing is farfetched. Pappenheim, after receiving the commission, went off to Traunkirchen to execute it, and it appears that the composer had little, if any, direct input in the formulation of the plot. Pappenheim delivered her first draft after three weeks, and Schoenberg was delighted. Although the poetess continued to fret and worry about her text, he seized upon it in its unperfected state and wrote the accompanying music in seventeen frenzied days.

Despite the uncanny parallels that exist between *Erwartung* and Schoenberg's personal life, it is evident that *Die glückliche Hand*, which he wrote himself, was a more explicit exploration of the Gerstl trauma. The fact that the composer sketched out the general idea of the work shortly before the painter took his life—and presumably just after Mathilde had returned to him—further supports this contention. Again there are striking parallels between the plot and Schoenberg's own story: the protagonist in *glückliche Hand* loses the woman he loves to a more elegant rival. She appears to return to him, and her encouragement endows him with magical powers. However, all is an illusion; the hero ends up as miserably as he began. Most of Schoenberg's text consists of elaborate stage directions (glowing hands and such), and there are a number of ponderous visual symbols, including a mythical beast that represents the hero's torment and a fragment torn from the heroine's dress to represent the piece of her heart that the rival still holds. Unlike Kokoschka's aggressive murderer, Schoenberg's "Man" is a victim of his own fate: of love, and of earthly desire.

Die glückliche Hand is not, however, only about unrequited love; it is also about the plight of the artist in society. The hero has extraordinary creative abilities—in one scene he is shown producing a diadem out of thin air—but he is vanquished by ordinary misfortune. The workers who witness his miraculous feat grumble suspiciously (much like Viennese concert audiences), and his lover is untrue. Only if, as the chorus tells him, he learns to stop yearning for the unattainable will he ever find peace: "Once again you give yourself up to the sirens of your thoughts, thoughts that roam the cosmos, that are unworldly but thirst for worldly fulfillment—you poor fool. Worldly fulfillment! You, who have the divine in you, and covet the worldly! And you cannot win out! You poor fool!"[38] Schoenberg, in composing *Glückliche Hand*, transformed his own story into a parable about the fate of the artist and by depersonalizing his suffering, was gradually able to overcome it.

Figure 16. Arnold Schoenberg: *Blue Self-Portrait*. **1910. Oil on wood. 12 1/4″ x 8 5/8″. (Schoenberg 5). Collection Lawrence and Ronald Schoenberg and Nuria Schoenberg Nono.**

THE PAINTINGS

Schoenberg's development of musical expressionism was closely paralleled by the advent of expressionism in the visual arts. This latter revolution had a relatively innocuous start with the founding of the Secession in 1897. Led by Gustav Klimt, the secessionists assumed their role reluctantly, breaking with the existing arts institution, the *Künstlerhaus*, only when that organization voted to censure them for attempting to foster reform within its ranks. The main problem with the *Künstlerhaus* was that its policy of majority rule tended to favor the more conservative elements. In truth, the original goals of the *Künstlerhaus*, founded in 1861, had been remarkably similar to those of the Secession: to combat what was regarded as the stagnation of Vienna's cultural institutions by providing young artists with more exposure, and to bring Vienna into closer contact with contemporary movements abroad. Within a year of its inception, the Secession was able to mount its first exhibition in rented space. By the end of 1898 it had moved into its own building, the rapid construction of which was facilitated by the support of wealthy patrons and the City of Vienna.

Innovators in the visual arts had access to more money than their counterparts in the field of music, but they were hardly treated more kindly by the press and general public. The first big scandal was occasioned not by the Secession itself, but rather by Klimt's painting *Philosophy* (Figure 17), which the Secession exhibited in 1900. *Philosophy* was commissioned by the University of Vienna, together with panels depicting the faculties of *Medicine* and *Jurisprudence*, the year after the Secession's founding. In executing this assignment, Klimt, influenced by the foreign symbolists whose work he had seen at the Secession, moved away from the prettified allegories that had previously won him general acclaim. Rather than an homage to the great philosophical tradition (how easy it would have been to simply crown Plato on a neoclassical throne), *Philosophy* focused on the human sorrows and passions that are the discipline's true subjects. The massing of intertwined human figures was not without precedent in Austrian mural painting,[1] but Klimt's use of total, undraped nudity, of frontal nudity, and perhaps worst of all, of ugly, unidealized nudity, broke every taboo.

The outcry provoked by the exhibition of *Philosophy* set the tone for the new century. Such a scandal, whose magnitude was similar to that of the 1874 impressionism debacle in Paris, had never before taken place in Vienna.[2] Because Klimt continued to work on the commission, exhibiting the second in the series, *Medicine*, in 1901, the furor did not abate. A group of professors at the university, some of whom had never seen Klimt's work, lodged a formal protest. The press reacted with typical rancor. "I beg you to try and think something sensible in front of this picture," one reviewer wrote of *Medicine*. "I can't—the walls are turning, and my stomach too. Help, where's the emergency exit?"[3] Klimt, thoroughly demoralized by the entire experience, eventually renounced the commission, completing the final panel, *Jurisprudence*, purely as a matter of personal pride. In a 1903 canvas, *The Battle of Life (The Golden Knight)* (Plate 3), he portrayed himself as lonely crusader, reflecting the involuntary martyrdom that was being foisted upon him.

Schoenberg, in the wake of such scandals, had sought succor from his circle of intimates; the secessionists had more powerful supporters, such as Hermann Bahr, and their own journal, *Ver Sacrum* (Sacred Spring), with which to counter the attacks of the tabloid press. Klimt's comrades rushed to defend him in print and in lectures. "If someone adopts the well-known and often heard expression 'I demand from the artist,' 'the artist should,' 'the artist must,' this proves that he has no idea of how the work of art comes into being," explained one of these writers. "He may approach the applied arts, which exist for his service, with such demands . . . . But no one in the world has any need of the work of art before it comes into being, with the exception of him who creates it."[4] This implicit distinction between the fine and the applied arts echoes surprisingly Loos's philosophy of architecture: "The work of art is the private affair of the artist. The house is not . . . . The work of art is answerable to no one; the house to everyone. The work of art wants to shake people out of their comfortableness. The house must serve comfort."[5] Despite his later disputes with Klimt, Loos was inclined to side with him in the university controversy. "In the case of Klimt," he wrote, "we see university professors and fishwives united behind the motto 'down with individuality.'"[6]

Problems developed between Klimt and Loos when the painter (and, more specifically, his collaborators) began to confuse the function of art with that of architecture. Klimt gradually rejected the moody symbolism of the university panels in favor of a more decorative approach, and in keeping with this change, he allied himself with the design-oriented members of the Secession. The founding of the *Wiener Werkstätte* in 1903 aggravated a growing rift between Klimt's faction and the conventional easel painters. In 1905 the so-called *Klimtgruppe* (Klimt Group), which included architects and designers such as Josef Hoffmann and Koloman Moser, seceded from the Secession. These artists all favored their own utilitarian interpretation of the *Gesamtkunstwerk* as a total living environment uniting the fine and applied arts. There is no doubt that the *Klimtgruppe* represented the most vital forces within the Secession, and when they departed, all that remained was a group of largely minor picture painters in an ornate picture palace. Klimt, left without a building, was in much the same position as he had been in 1897. Using rented space, he and his colleagues mounted their first exhibition, the *Kunstschau* (Art Show) in 1908. "There is no aspect of culture," Klimt stated in his opening address, "that is so insignificant and trifling that it does not offer room for artistic endeavor."[7] "Art," retorted Loos, "will now be squandered on tin cans and bracelets. These times are worse than we think."[8]

The 1908 *Kunstschau*, however, was not all ornament and dross. Among the baubles and bedsteads was a small room, immediately dubbed the "Chamber of Horrors" by the

Figure 17. Gustav Klimt: *Philosophy*. **1899-1907. Oil on canvas. 169 1/4″ x 118 1/8″. (Novotny/Dobai 105). Destroyed.**

Figure 18. Oskar Kokoschka: *The Girl Li and I.* 1906–08. Color lithograph. 9 1/2" x 11 3/8". Illustration from "Die träumenden Knaben." (Wingler/Welz 29).

Figure 19. Oskar Kokoschka: *Male Nude and Female Nude, Seated.* 1914. Lithograph. 9 1/2" x 6 1/4". Illustration from "Allos Makar." (Wingler/Welz 69).

ever eloquent press, in which a young student at the School of Applied Art, Oskar Kokoschka, exhibited his work for the first time. The protests seem to have been triggered primarily by a garishly painted portrait bust into whose gaping mouth bits of candy and debris were daily placed by the taunting visitors. Since this sculpture, and also four controversial tapestry designs executed for the artist's part-time employer, the *Wiener Werkstätte*, no longer exist, it is difficult to judge the extremity of Kokoschka's contribution. The remainder of his work was strictly in line with that of his colleagues at school and the *Wiener Werkstätte*. His "children's" book, *Die träumenden Knaben* (The Dreaming Boys), for example, is, in retrospect, deemed protoexpressionistic more on the basis of its idiosyncratic text than for the stylistic characteristics of the illustrations (Figure 18). It is indicative of Kokoschka's artistic loyalties that he dedicated the book to Klimt, whom he had not yet met,[9] and also that he (unlike Gerstl) contributed willingly to the 1908 *Festzug.* Kokoschka's brother Bohuslav has said that Gerstl tried to contact Oskar after the *Kunstschau,*[10] but it is doubtful that even if he succeeded, the meeting had any significance, for Gerstl's work had already reached expressive extremes that the other painter would never equal. Nevertheless, the irksome portrait bust—which Kokoschka had modeled on the warrior masks in Vienna's ethnographic museum rather than on any established fine arts precedent—transcended everything else that he and the other *Kunstschau* artists had done. To Loos it seemed to offer a way out of the decorative morass into which Viennese art was sinking, and so he acquired it for his collection.

In 1909 Klimt and his cohorts mounted a second *Kunstschau*, which, unlike the first, was international in scope, including works by, among others, Van Gogh, Gauguin, Munch, Vlaminck, and Matisse. Van Gogh had been the subject of a highly acclaimed exhibition at Miethke in 1906, but the progressive exhibition program of the Secession had more or less ended with the exodus of the *Klimtgruppe* in 1905. For the younger Viennese artists—and this included both Kokoschka and Egon Schiele—the second *Kunstschau* was probably their first exposure to modern European art. This time Schiele joined Kokoschka in the *"Wildenkabinett"* (Savage Section), exhibiting works perhaps radical for the day, but still clearly bearing the stylistic stamp of his mentor Gustav Klimt. Kokoschka showed an oil portrait and another portrait bust in which the expressionistic promise of his earlier work was more clearly realized, but also a number of fairly typical *Wiener Werkstätte* designs, including drawings for a never published follow-up to *Die träumenden Knaben*, *Der weisse Tiertöter* (The White Animal Slayer). Though expressionism was latent in the work of both artists, neither entirely renounced the more decorative or Klimtian aspects of his style until after the *Kunstschau*. Of the two, Kokoschka was the more advanced, and it is likely that Schiele was encouraged by his example as well as by that of some of the foreign painters in the exhibition.

In the case of Kokoschka, it is clear that Loos provided the decisive push in the direction of expressionism. The second *Kunstschau* had confirmed his initial assessment of Kokoschka's potential, and Loos vowed that he would not allow such talent to go to waste. As he later recounted:

> I was told that he was an employee of the *Wiener Werkstätte* and was busying himself painting fans, designing postcards and such things in the German [i.e., Jugendstil] manner—art in the service of commerce. It was immediately clear to me that a great crime against the Holy Ghost was being perpetrated here. So I summoned him. He came....I promised him the same income, if he would leave the *Wiener Werkstätte*, and I sought commissions for him.[11]

On the occasion of Loos's sixtieth birthday, Kokoschka acknowledged his profound debt to the architect: "You took me out of my environment, alienating me from the present and, thereby, imbued me with a greater life, a life in a higher sense. You are my spiritual foster-father."[12]

Kokoschka, as a student at the School of Applied Art, had not trained in the fine arts, and it was his stated ambition to become not an artist, but an art teacher. Loos, however, soon made good his promise and began to get the fledgling painter portrait commissions. Kokoschka, in turn, began to devote his full attention to working on canvas, something he had not done before. His first paintings must be considered, to a certain extent, the efforts of an autodidact. Experimental in nature, the portraits violated all existing conventions: both those that were taught at the conservative Academy of Fine Art and those that had been more recently established by Klimt. In technique, too, the paintings were unorthodox. Instead of building form through the application of progressive layers of pigment, Kokoschka used a palette knife to remove paint, exposing raw swathes of canvas or incising the paint surface with electric little lines. In the process, he also laid bare the souls of his sitters, producing portraits of exceptional intensity (Plates 20 and 21).

For Schiele, too, the 1909 *Kunstschau* was a decisive experience. Bolstered by the thrill of his first significant public showing, and by Klimt's encouragement, he decided to drop out of the Academy of Fine Art, where he, like Gerstl, had been subjected to the tortures of Herr Professor Griepenkerl. Mindful of the Austrian propensity for christening artistic allegiances with an organizational name, he gathered a coterie of like-minded students into something called the *Neukunstgruppe* (New Art Group), which exhibited at the Pisko Salon at the end of the year. Schiele's style (Figure 22)—his obsession with anatomical rendering and his elegant use of line—betrayed the influence both of his academic background and his enduring ties to Klimt (Figures 20 and 21). As a consequence, his drawing technique, even at its most erratic, eschewed the angular, antinaturalistic qualities of Kokoschka's. Schiele retained the belief that drawing is the skeleton on which painting rests, and whereas Kokoschka's paintings grew spontaneously from his manipulation of pigment, Schiele's had a strong, linear structure. His expressionism was not the expressionism of the primitive, but rather an evolutionary exploration of the human emotive potential latent in Klimt's suggestive symbolism.

Neither Schiele nor Kokoschka could have seen Gerstl's work, which after his death was consigned to a dusty warehouse for twenty-three years.[13] Schoenberg, on the other hand, was unable to forget the young painter. In 1908, six weeks after the suicide, he created his first dated painting. Within the next two years, he would execute approximately two-thirds of a total oeuvre comprising about sixty-five oils.[14] Many have speculated on the reasons why the composer chose to experiment with a new medium. Why paint? And why at this particular moment in his life? According to Victor Hammer, it was Gerstl who first instructed Schoenberg (and also his wife Mathilde) in the use of paint. Yet even assuming this to be true, Schoenberg's sporadic efforts prior to 1908 can hardly compare with his all-out pursuit of painting in the ensuing years. Given the pain engendered by the entire Gerstl episode, one might have expected Schoenberg to stay as far away from painters and painting as possible. The fact that just the opposite was the case suggests that the composer may subconsciously have turned to painting as a way to confront and overcome his anguish. It was a remedy akin to the old wives' cure of swallowing "a hair of the dog that bit you."

The convergence of Schoenberg's career as a painter with his emancipation of dissonance and his experiments in theater may also be significant. As Jelena Hahl-Koch has pointed out, artists frequently turn to an unfamiliar medium when their own work has reached a moment of crisis or transition. At a certain stage, the artist's intimate knowledge of his primary medium may become an obstacle to transcending its limits, whereas a new medium offers greater freedom from convention. This explanation may be applied to Kandinsky's and Kokoschka's theatrical works as well as to Schoenberg's, for each of these men had reached a turning point in his work by 1908 or 1909. Moreover, it was then standard practice for avant-garde artists to dismiss the validity of formal education. This being the case, it was easy to assume that a painter was no more or less qualified to write plays than a playwright, or that a composer, given the inclination, could paint

Figure 20. Gustav Klimt: *Seated Woman*. Ca. 1907-08. Pencil and red crayon on simile Japan paper. (Strobl 1697). 20 7/8″ x 13 7/8″. Collection Mrs. Alice M. Kaplan.

Figure 21. Gustav Klimt: *Lovers*. Ca. 1915. Pencil on simile Japan paper. 22 1/4″ x 14 3/4″. Private collection.

Figure 22. Egon Schiele: *Reclining Woman*. 1918. Charcoal on yellowish paper. 11 3/4″ x 18 1/8″. Private collection.

just as well as a school-trained artist. Schoenberg, after all, had practically taught himself to compose. Why, then, *not* paint?

There is yet another reason why, at this critical moment in his life, Schoenberg may have turned to painting. He had accepted the break with tonality as his fate. The concerts of 1907 and 1908 amply demonstrated the Viennese response to works that preceded this development; he could well anticipate the reaction to his new, "atonal" compositions. In keeping with his unenviable reputation, his income from composing was as pitiful as it had ever been; indeed, to call him a "professional" composer would almost be a cruel joke. Without suggesting that Schoenberg ever considered abandoning music— for this he clearly could not have done—it is conceivable that he contemplated a dual career as a composer/painter.

Early in 1910, Schoenberg's financial situation took a turn for the worse. In desperation, he wrote to Emil Hertzka, the director of Universal Edition, with a novel suggestion:

> You know that I paint. What you do not know is that my work is highly praised by experts. And I am to have an exhibition next year. What I have in mind is that you might be able to get one or another well-known patron to buy some of my pictures or have his portrait done by me.[15]

Apparently Hertzka did not take Schoenberg's proposal very seriously, and the exhibition plans referred to in this letter seem to have fallen through.[16] Therefore, in June 1910 the composer asked his friend Carl Moll to arrange a show at the Galerie Miethke, which Moll served as artistic advisor. Moll rejected the idea in polite but firm terms:

> I can tell from your work that you have an excellent color sense; that you have something to say both as a man and as an artist has long been evident. My pedestrian opinion, however, is that one must express oneself in an artistic manner if one wishes to address the public. Your manner of artistic expression as a painter appears to me to be very much in the beginning stages—I also fear that your hopes with regard to the material prospects will not be realized if you make the wrong move.[17]

Schoenberg was not daunted by Moll's opinion, and in October 1910 an exhibition of forty-two[18] works was sponsored by the book and art dealer Hugo Heller. The fact that the majority of Schoenberg's dated paintings were done in 1910 suggests that the desire to exhibit, and the anticipated monetary rewards, were a prime motivating factor for him.

That Schoenberg could have expected the public who hissed and walked out at his concerts to line up to buy his paintings indicates how truly naive he was when it came to the art world and how relatively remote from that world he must have been. Perhaps he was unaware of the art scandals of the last decade, or if not, he nonetheless made no connection between them and himself. The press lit into him with characteristic verve. "Now he paints," began one reviewer. "From the first glance it is terrible. One recoils in horror."[19] Members of the Court Opera joked, "Schoenberg's music and Schoenberg's pictures—that will knock your ears and eyes out at the same time."[20] Three paintings were sold—all, as it turned out years later, to Gustav Mahler, who bought them anonymously to help his friend.

Despite the judgment of the press and public (whom Schoenberg had long ago learned to dismiss as imbeciles), it is clear that the composer placed great value on his paintings. In his letter to Hertzka, he wrote:

> You must not tell people that they *will* like my pictures. You must make them realize that they cannot but like my pictures, because they have been praised by authorities on painting, and above all, that it is much more interesting to have one's portrait done or to own a painting by a musician of my reputation than to be painted by some mere practitioner of painting whose name will be forgotten in twenty years; whereas even now my name belongs to the history of music. For a life-size portrait I want from two to six sittings and 200 to 400 kronen. That is really very cheap, considering that in twenty years people will pay ten times as much and in forty years a hundred times as much for these paintings.[21]

Judging from the above, it is conceivable that Schoenberg's painting career was in part frustrated by unrealistic prices. Schiele, at the start of his career, asked between 60 and 150 kronen for an oil, and one of Kokoschka's early portrait commissions went begging at 200 kronen. When Schiele raised his prices to 300-400 kronen in 1912, he was reproached for exceeding the limits of the market. Kokoschka was able to raise his prices only gradually, after a series of successful exhibitions.[22] Schoenberg, relying on his somewhat questionable reputation as a composer, completely ignored the fact that he had no standing whatsoever as a painter and expected to receive prices that were acceptable only for established artists. He did not understand that painters, just like composers, have to nurture a following for their work before they can expect to be well paid for it.

In a peculiar way (and, in part, probably because he was unfamiliar with the art market), Schoenberg valued his paintings above his music. In the mid 1940s, when he was living in the United States, he priced the complete forty-eight-page score of *Pierrot Lunaire*, one of his acknowledged masterpieces, at $1,500; for the painting *Tears* (Cover), he wanted more than twice that, $3,500, and for a self-portrait, $5,000.[23] Again, by way of comparison, good-sized oils by Schiele brought $1,500 at the time, and even Kokoschka, who was better known in America, commanded prices that were scarcely higher; a Renoir could be had for between $2,000 and $4,000. Toward the end of his life, Schoenberg considered his paintings an important component—perhaps the most important component—of his legacy. In 1949 he declined an invitation to exhibit in Germany, saying, "The risk of losing the pictures is graver for me than for a museum. For a museum it is just one of the pieces they have; for me it is—let us be quite frank about it—what I intend to leave to my heirs, hoping that someday it will bring them a sum worth having."[24] At no point in his life had Schoenberg been able to live off the income produced by his compositions, and he had no reason to expect that his heirs would do any better. To make matters worse, he complained that the value of his musical copyrights would be diminished by the terms of U.S. law, which, unlike its European counterpart, measures the duration of copyright from the date of a work's creation rather than from the date of the artist's death. Consequently, the paintings were among his most tangible assets.

Beyond any monetary value that Schoenberg ascribed to the paintings, it must be said that he believed in them as art, and that he turned to painting primarily because he viewed it as a valid creative outlet. Painting, he insisted, "was the same to me as making music. It was to me a way of expressing myself, of presenting emotions, ideas and other feelings."[25] He derived the same satisfaction from painting as from composing, experienced the same intuitive thrill that told him, *"It is good."* As he went on to explain to the dubious Carl Moll:

> I must believe: *this is something*. At first glance it must seem strange that I assume that someone who can do nothing is suddenly capable of doing something. However, I do not consider this unusual; it is with me, in any event, routinely the case. *I have always been able to do only that which is suited to me—absolutely, immediately* and almost without any *transition* or preparation. On the other hand, the things that others can do—that which passes for "education"—have always caused me difficulties. I have also mastered them. But only later. Only after I have struggled through to a certain security in my natural domain, did I also acquire the power to do what the others could.[26]

In judging Schoenberg's paintings, it is important to bear in mind that the artist was self-taught and, also, that he was not, first and foremost, a painter. Like many so-called "naive" artists, he came to his task full-blown, and some of his earliest paintings are actually more competent than the rather dilettantish portraits and cartoons he did later. Because he never substantially altered his initial vision, he had no stylistic development in the usual sense. "As a painter I was absolutely an amateur," he explained. "I had no theoretical training and only a little aesthetic training, and this only from general education, but not from an education which pertained to painting. In music it was different. So I was also an...autodidact. I had always had the opportunity to study the works of the masters and to study them in quite a professional manner, so that my technical ability grew in the normal manner. That is the difference between my painting and my music."[27]

Schoenberg, then, did not look at paintings in quite the same way that an artist usually does: he did not study technical nuance or attempt to understand the grand sweep of tradition with the intention of incorporating these observations in his work. Beyond the mere fact of lacking conventional artistic training, he lacked the conventional artist's approach to art. This point becomes crucial when one considers the question of influence, for if one accepts that Schoenberg did not view painting as a normal artist does, one must accept the fact that the concept of influence, at least in the usual sense, is irrelevant.

Schoenberg himself fumed at his biographers for suggesting that he could have been influenced by any other artist:

> This is the way their brain [sic] works:
> 1) Schoenberg composed something original
> 2) therefore it is not by him (without statement of reasons)
> 3) he gets it from somebody else[28]

Schoenberg objected to this insinuation not merely because it called into question his originality, but because it was a slur on his integrity as an artist. Painting was not just a casual hobby or affectation, but an authentic representation of his innermost self. ''I called it 'making music in colors and forms,''' he once explained, ''and this only I could do.'' [29] Because he had not studied the work of other painters, but only painted what he felt intuitively, he thought it slander of a most callous sort to attribute his innovations to anyone else.

Of course, one cannot deny that Schoenberg was familiar with Gerstl's work. More difficult to determine is whether he was aware of general artistic developments taking place in Vienna. Of the twenty or so exhibition catalogues in his library, about half stem from the period between 1908 and 1912, the earliest being the catalogue for the first *Kunstschau*. One may infer from this that he attended one, if not both, of the two *Kunstschauen*, and he also seems to have followed, at least sporadically, developments at the Galerie Miethke.[30] He was partial to Klimt (Webern gave him a portfolio of reproductions for his forty-seventh birthday), and therefore obviously did not make the same distinction that Gerstl, Kokoschka, and, to a lesser extent, Schiele did between the ''old'' art and the ''new.'' Berg once created a flowery Art Nouveau cover for a Schoenberg score, again suggesting that radical music did not necessarily demand equally radical artistic tastes. A curious set of playing cards designed by Schoenberg in the *Jugendstil* manner is the only indication that he himself ever indulged in this type of art.[31] The rest of his work is clearly in line with the general expressionist trend.

In judging potential influences, the question of who knew whom, when, remains critical. To some extent, liasons can be traced through the existence of portraits: Kokoschka painted Webern in 1914 and drew him in 1912. Mopp painted Webern in 1910, and Schoenberg in 1909. There is little doubt that by 1911 the composer was quite friendly with both artists as well as with Loos, Kraus, and Altenberg. He had known Loos perhaps as early as 1904, had been a devoted reader of *Die Fackel* for years, knew Mopp through Berg, and had met Kokoschka in 1909. Yet the questions still remain: To what extent was Schoenberg on intimate terms with these people prior to 1910, and, more important, to what extent did he concern himself with their ideas about the visual arts? Did his exhibition in 1910 draw him closer to Loos's circle, or did a preexisting relationship with this group prompt him to take his painting more seriously?

Schoenberg's emergence as a painter coincides so closely with Kokoschka's and Schiele's first expressionist works that the question of influence seems almost beside the point. Certainly the composer began painting before there had been any public manifestations of expressionism. Schiele exhibited his first expressionistic paintings at Miethke in 1910, and Kokoschka did not have his first important Viennese show until 1911. Of the two artists, it is likely that Schoenberg was only interested in Kokoschka at this time, for they were joined by their mutual association with men such as Loos and Mopp. Schiele, who had been a student at the Academy of Fine Art, moved in different social circles from Kokoschka, (in fact, according to Kokoschka, the two never met),[32] and his ongoing relationship with Klimt precluded an alliance with the Loos camp.

It appears that Schoenberg was initially attracted to Kokoschka as a writer rather than as a painter. This may be because, in the summer of 1909, Kokoschka's expressionistic tendencies were more clearly manifested in his plays, or it may have been that the plays were more relevant to the composer's immediate interests at the time. In any case, toward

Figure 23. Gustav Klimt: *Pine Forest II*. 1901. Oil on canvas. 35 1/2" x 35 1/2". (Novotny/Dobai 121). Private collection.

the end of 1909, shortly after they met, Kokoschka went to Switzerland on a portrait-painting mission. Upon his return, he moved to Berlin. Schoenberg's relationship with the painter was curtailed by these events, but it is nonetheless possible that he saw Kokoschka's 1909-10 portraits of his acquaintances Loos, Altenberg, and Kraus. Still, considering that just about everyone Loos knew was having his portrait done by Kokoschka, it is curious that Schoenberg does not figure among the sitters. Perhaps the composer was not yet so close to Loos, or maybe he was excluded because he could not afford to pay for such a luxury. Whether or not he knew the portraits, the fact that Kokoschka was being commissioned to paint them and was being supported by the likes of Loos must have encouraged Schoenberg to pursue his artistic ambitions. To the extent that he was aware of the work of the fledgling expressionists, he could not but have sensed an affinity between it and his own.

Figure 24. Richard Gerstl: *Small Traunsee Landscape*. **Ca. 1907-08. Oil on canvas, mounted on cardboard. 15 7/8″ x 14 1/4″. (Kallir 11). Private collection.**

Without becoming embroiled in what has long been an unresolved art-historical debate, it may be said that "expressionism" can be loosely defined as a term referring to art that is in some way directly expressive of human emotion as filtered through the personal perceptions of the artist. Schoenberg's music and Schoenberg's paintings can both be called expressionistic, as can the work of Gerstl, Kokoschka, and Schiele. Yet beyond this broad generalization, each artist defined his task in a somewhat different manner. Furthermore, the expressionism of Schoenberg's music was quite different from that of his paintings, for as we have seen, he was a professional in one and an amateur in the other.

Gerstl, the first Austrian expressionist, was the only one of his compatriots who made a deliberate attempt to come to terms with the legacy of French impressionism. This is

Figure 25. Arnold Schoenberg: *Night Landscape*. 1910. Oil on canvas. 22 7/8" x 28 3/4". (Schoenberg 140). Collection Lawrence and Ronald Schoenberg and Nuria Schoenberg Nono.

not surprising, as he is the only one of the group likely to have seen the Secession's 1903 impressionism survey (which also included works by Gauguin and Van Gogh). Schiele, at the time, was still a boy attending *Gymnasium* (the Austrian equivalent of high school) in the Vienna suburb of Klosterneuburg. Kokoschka had not yet passed his *Matura* (the final exam given at the conclusion of *Gymnasium*) and, by his own account, did not take much interest in art exhibitions. Though both would eventually absorb foreign influences, particularly in the aftermath of the 1909 *Kunstschau*, their chief point of reference was Klimt's Art Nouveau and its various offshoots. Whatever initial contact they had with French modernism was filtered through Klimt, but they responded more obviously to the aspects of his work that derived from international symbolism. Thus they were both

Figure 26. Arnold Schoenberg: *Landscape*. **Oil on cardboard. 19 1/4" x 19 5/8". (Schoenberg 143). Collection Lawrence and Ronald Schoenberg and Nuria Schoenberg Nono.**

concerned with expressing human themes, and unlike artists who had more contact with the French (Gerstl and Kandinsky among them), they did not develop in the direction of abstraction.

Gerstl's interest in French formalist aesthetics manifests itself most clearly in his heightened awareness of the presence of the picture plane and its relationship to paint surface. Surprisingly (considering his professed hatred of the Viennese master), it is this aspect of Gerstl's work that is closest to Klimt's. Particularly in their landscapes (Figures 23 and 24), both artists favored an all-over treatment of the canvas that verges on total abstraction. However, whereas Klimt dissolved his subjects in a web of paint to achieve a feeling of serenity, in Gerstl's work the effect is just the opposite. Klimt's 1910 paint-

Figure 27. Richard Gerstl: *Group Portrait (The Arnold Schoenberg Family)*. **Oil on canvas. 66 3/8″ x 43 1/8″. (Kallir 49). Private collection.**

ing *The Black Feather Hat* (Plate 4) reveals how he chose to come to terms with the contribution of French artists such as Toulouse-Lautrec; foreground and background merge, and as already implied by the impersonal title, the identity of the sitter is obscured by the formal interplay of the essentially monochromatic brushstrokes. In Gerstl's painting of a similar subject (Plate 5), the small, erratic brushstrokes animate the form, conveying a sense of nervous anticipation that is quite at odds with the sitter's elegant demeanor. The conventions of the society portrait are violated, not through formal dematerialization, as in the Klimt, but through the aggressive intrusion of the painter's own personality. Gerstl's use of pointillism in this and other works from the same period (Figure 1) proved crucial to his future development. Unlike the French post-impressionists, whose manner he had adopted, he did not employ the colored dots merely to represent the effects of light, but rather exploited the method's expressive potential. To the precision of the technique as originally formulated, he wedded the broad impasto of the so-called German impressionists, Lovis Corinth and Max Liebermann, creating a unique hybrid.

Few of Gerstl's paintings are dated, and so it is possible to posit only a hypothetical developmental sequence. As Schoenberg tells us, when they met, Gerstl's style could hardly be considered radical by today's standards. "His ideal," scoffed the composer, "was Liebermann."[33] One can imagine that when Schoenberg began to paint, Gerstl was intrigued by the naive directness of his vision, which reaffirmed his own ongoing attempts to break free of convention. "Now I have learned from you how one has to paint!" he exclaimed.[34] Yet it is likely that Gerstl learned as much, or more, from Schoenberg's musical creations as he did from his pictures. Schoenberg's painstaking efforts to work his way through and beyond tradition in these seminal years immediately preceding the tonal rupture more clearly paralleled Gerstl's own attempts to assimilate the heritage of his artistic forebears. Gerstl, who had no mentor in the visual arts, identified with Schoenberg's loyal little circle, and the style that he perfected during that last fateful summer in Gmunden owes much to his association with them. He had begun to find the uniformity of the pointillist scheme inhibiting; the brushstrokes would be more effective if each were different. In his final portraits of the Schoenberg group (Figure 27), the identities of the subjects are all but obliterated by the vigorous presence of the brushwork. By fragmenting form (that is, creating surface disunity), he permitted each component element (that is, each brushstroke) to assume an independent expressive identity. It was the pictorial equivalent of emancipating dissonance.

Whether or not Gerstl gave Schoenberg painting lessons (and, in truth, the composer never actually denied this), the painter's path through tradition to the final "emancipation" of brushstroke was one that the composer, as an uneducated amateur, could not exactly follow. Gerstl, like any artist, was concerned with creating a total composition, and arrayed his subject on the canvas accordingly. Before venturing into abstraction, he had mastered the rudiments of human anatomy, and even his most advanced paintings are all solidly grounded in this academic knowledge. Schoenberg, on the other hand, had little grasp of anatomy; he had trouble with the human figure and usually managed to avoid it. For the most part, he was content to confine his scope to faces, which he simply plopped in the center of the canvas. As a result, the pictures become extremely quiet; with no distracting compositional activity, the viewer's attention is held simply by the magnetic

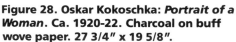

Figure 28. Oskar Kokoschka: _Portrait of a Woman_. Ca. 1920-22. Charcoal on buff wove paper. 27 3/4" x 19 5/8".

Figure 29. Oskar Kokoschka: _Mary Mersen, Seated_. 1931. Sanguine on cream wove paper. 22" x 17 1/2".

power of the eyes (Plate 1). Stylistically, his paintings bear little resemblance to those of Gerstl: the paint surfaces are fairly smooth, not heavily impastoed; the atmosphere is calm, not violent.

The effects of Schoenberg's lack of formal training are most visible in his portraits and self-portraits, whose rigid frontality and lack of compositional grace distinguish them not only from the work of Gerstl, but also from that of Kokoschka and Schiele. As he himself admitted, his work was "completely contrary to the nature of a real painter."[35] While the placement of a portrait subject in a compositional void was a device used by many expressionists to focus attention on the personality of the sitter, these "professionals" differed from Schoenberg in their articulation of the negative space in which the sitter was placed. The inherent contradiction between the two-dimensional compositional plane and the three-dimensional figure, which added an element of tension to the portraits of Gerstl and the others, was something Schoenberg could not master. At his most successful, he let his subject simply melt into the background (Plate 24).

Figure 31. Arnold Schoenberg: *Portrait*. **Pencil on off-white wove paper. 4" x 3 3/8". (Schoenberg 114). Collection Lawrence and Ronald Schoenberg and Nuria Schoenberg Nono.**

Figure 30. Arnold Schoenberg: *Portrait*. **Purple crayon on cream wove paper. 15 5/8" x 11 1/2". (Schoenberg 99). Collection Lawrence and Ronald Schoenberg and Nuria Schoenberg Nono.**

Schoenberg comes closest to his academically educated contemporaries in his drawings (Figures 30 and 31). Using media—pencil, charcoal, ink and pastel—that are simpler and more easily controlled than oil, he achieved greater technical facility while, conversely, his counterparts exploited the spontaneity of the same media to create drawings (Figures 28 and 29) that were looser and somewhat less "finished" than their oils. Consequently, their drawings and Schoenberg's meet halfway between primitivism and sophistication. Schoenberg's tendency to treat landscapes (Figures 25 and 26) in terms of flat planes also invites comparison with the professionals, particularly with Gerstl and Klimt, as does the surprising appearance of a pseudopointillist technique (Plate 26). However, the composer's most direct link to the other Austrian expressionists is not stylistic but thematic.

Whether or not they were familiar with Freud's recently published writings on the subconscious, Austrian artists in the early twentieth century perceived exploration of the self as a primary aesthetic mission. "Art belongs to the *unconscious*," Schoenberg vehemently declared. "One must express oneself *directly*. Not one's taste, or one's upbring-

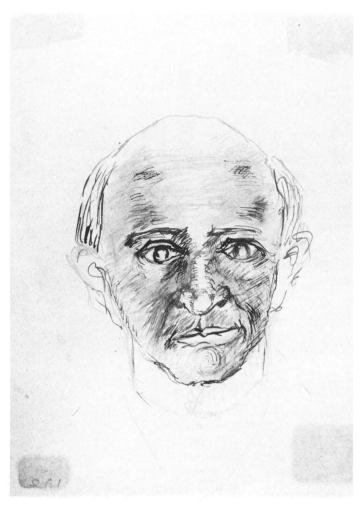

Figure 32. Arnold Schoenberg: *Self-Portrait*. **Pen and blue and black ink on cream wove paper. 5 3/8″ x 4 1/4″. (Schoenberg 39). Collection Lawrence and Ronald Schoenberg and Nuria Schoenberg Nono.**

Figure 33. Egon Schiele: *Study for the Portrait of Eduard Kosmak*. **1910. Charcoal, watercolor, and gouache on brown paper. 17 1/2″ x 12″. Collection Mrs. Alice M. Kaplan.**

ing, or one's intelligence, knowledge or skill. Not all these acquired characteristics, but that which is *inborn, instinctive.*"[36] The artist's personality was so pivotal to the concept of expressionism that one might almost say that "self-" is the term's unenunciated prefix. These artists believed that they could see through the self to some greater truth, that their struggles and feelings could somehow be communicated to others. Schiele created a number of mystical self-portraits with titles such as *Self-Seers* (Figure 34) or, more simply, *Vision*, and Kokoschka attempted to transform personal experience into a universal paradigm by executing a cycle of allegorical illustrations depicting his stormy relationship with Alma Mahler (Figure 19). In the symbolic representations of the expressionists, the broad human truths that had been hinted at in Klimt's university allegories were, quite literally, given faces. And more often than not, it was the face of the artist himself.

Figure 34. Egon Schiele: *The Self-Seers I*. **1910. Oil on canvas. 31 1/2″ x 31 3/8″. (Kallir 113). Whereabouts unknown.**

It is no accident, then, that most of the Austrian painters showed an unusual preoccupation with self-portraiture. It has been remarked that even their portraits of others are, in a sense, self-portraits, for the painter's identification with the sitter is such that the artist's personality, rather than the sitter's, becomes the dominant element. Schoenberg recognized this when he wrote, "Who, a hundred years hence, will be able to judge the resemblance? — but the artistic effect will always remain, and this is so because we are addressed not by a real man, the apparent subject of the portrait, but rather by the artist, who, having expressed himself in the portrait, must be considered its true subject."[37] Self-portraiture consumes approximately one-fifth of Schoenberg's oeuvre. Kokoschka, too, created a number of eloquent self-portraits (Plate 9), and Schiele and Gerstl both had ongoing relationships with the large mirrors that were dominant fixtures

Figure 35. Arnold Schoenberg: *Self-Portrait*. **Pastel on cream wove paper. 13 3/4" x 11 7/8". (Schoenberg 45). Collection Lawrence and Ronald Schoenberg and Nuria Schoenberg Nono.**

Figure 36. Richard Gerstl: *Self-Portrait*. **1908. Wash, pen and ink, and charcoal on ivory paper. 15 3/4" x 11 5/8". (Kallir 63). Estate of Otto Kallir.**

Figure 37. Egon Schiele: *Self-Portrait*. **1912. Pencil and watercolor on buff wove paper. 13 3/4" x 10". Private collection.**

in their studios. Each of the latter two artists painted himself nude with a frankness that, at the time, made the results impossible to exhibit. They also explored every detail of their faces: the youthful bravado, the lingering doubts (Figure 37), and, in the case of Gerstl, the gradual descent into despair and madness (Figure 36).

In contrast to the excruciatingly personal self-representations of Kokoschka, Schiele, and Gerstl, Schoenberg's self-portraits (Figure 35) are relatively opaque. They do not particularly speak of any one time or place, nor, when compared with photographs of the composer (Figures 51 and 52) do they evidence any noticeable signs of aging. Although Eberhard Freitag finds certain symptoms of insecurity in some of the drawings done in America, the fact remains that in most of Schoenberg's self-portraits we are given little clue as to the artist's emotional state. Was he happy or sad, angry or pleased? No; he was, quite simply, Arnold Schoenberg. Unlike the other expressionists, he was less concerned with portraying transitory states than with capturing some inner essence that was unchanging. In this, he formulated a somewhat different concept of self-expressionism than that practiced by Kokoschka or Schiele. To arrive at the subconscious in art, he reasoned, one would have to eliminate the conscious will. Kokoschka and Schiele, on the other hand, felt that the inner spirit could be expressed only through a highly refined consciousness of self. The difference was that between the dream itself and the dream as examined on the analyst's couch.

Schoenberg made a distinction between the bulk of his portraits, which he likened to "finger exercises" or "scales," and his "Visions" or "Gazes" (or, as he preferred to call them, the "Impressions" and "Fantasies")[38] "I never saw faces," he explained, "but, because I looked into people's eyes, only their 'gazes.' This is why I can imitate the gaze of a person. A painter, however, grasps with one look the whole person—I only his soul."[39] This preoccupation with "gazes" was not as unique as Schoenberg believed. The burning stare of Schiele's *Eduard Kosmak* (Figure 33), like the eyes of almost all the expressionist portraits, were the focus of the picture, the living spiritual presence behind often worn and sagging flesh. As Kokoschka put it, the eyes were "the window of a brain whose intelligence I was trying to portray."[40] It is no coincidence that Kokoschka titled his first theoretical essay, written in 1912, "On the Nature of Visions" and wrote that "things end up with no existence beyond my inner vision of them."[41] Vision as an artistic process—the attempt to record not the thing seen so much as the act of seeing—was a concept much in vogue at the turn of the century. Although its implications could be purely optical, as they were in the more formalistic interpretations, for the Austrians the presence of the artistic consciousness was the primary expressive component of vision.

While Schoenberg recognized that his portraits bore the telltale stamp of his amateur status, he valued the "Visions" as true art. In these works, the face itself tends to merge with the background in a soft haze of color (Plate 25). The harmonies are muted, almost nonexistent. Schoenberg did not know how to bounce contrasting colors off each other for heightened expressive effect (as Gerstl or any professional artist would), but he did know how, subtly, to tune them to the same pitch so that they would set up an almost imperceptible vibration, an atmosphere in which the eyes could hover. At times the ripples in this surface vibration are so minimal that the subject vanishes altogether. Perhaps because he was an amateur, Schoenberg had the courage to paint the unpaintable, and some of his depictions of mental states such as *Thinking* are among the first entirely abstract works ever created. Gerstl never became truly abstract, and Kandinsky (Figure 39) executed his first abstract paintings only around 1913.[42] Schoenberg probably painted *Thinking* and other works like it before he met Kandinsky. However, when he first saw photographs of Kandinsky's work in early 1911, he immediately recognized a kindred spirit. "I myself don't believe that painting must necessarily be objective," the composer declared.

> Indeed, I firmly believe the contrary. Nevertheless, when the imagination suggests objective things to us, then, well and good—perhaps that is because our eyes perceive only objective things. The ear has an advantage in this regard! But when the artist reaches the point at which he desires only the expression of inner events and inner scenes in his rhythms and tones, then the "object in painting" has ceased to belong to the reproducing eye.[43]

Kandinsky was instinctively attracted to Schoenberg, whose work he first heard performed at a Munich concert on New Years's day in 1911. Like Gerstl, he sensed in the music a corollary to, and hence justification for, what he was trying to achieve. "The independent progress through their own destinies, the independent life of the individual voices in your compositions, is exactly what I am trying to find in my painting," he exulted.[44] Kandinsky immediately initiated a correspondence with the composer and soon became a fan of his pictures as well:

> First of all, we see immediately that Schoenberg paints not in order to paint something "beautiful" or "engaging," but that he paints without even thinking about the painting itself. Renouncing the objective result, he seeks to affix only his subjective feelings, and uses for that purpose only the means which seem to him indispensable at that moment. Not every professional artist can lay claim to this mode of creativity! Or, stated differently, infinitely few professional artists possess this fortunate power, and at times this heroism, this energy of renunciation, whereby all kinds of artistic diamonds and pearls, when they fall of themselves into their hands, are quietly left aside or even discarded. Schoenberg proceeds directly toward his goal, directly toward the necessary resolution.... We see that in every painting by Schoenberg, the inner wish of the artist speaks in the form which best befits it. Just as in his music...Schoenberg also in his painting renounces the superfluous (therefore the harmful) and proceeds along a direct path to the essential (therefore to the necessary).[45]

Contrary to what one might expect, judging from Kandinsky's own work, it was not Schoenberg's mystical "Visions" and "Gazes" that caught his fancy, but the more awkward "finger exercises." When he began corresponding with the composer, Kandinsky was in the process of refining the aesthetic theories that in 1912 would be published in his book *On the Spiritual in Art* and in the *Blaue Reiter* Almanac, the journal of the so-called *Blaue Reiter* artists, who included Alfred Kubin, Gabriele Münter, and Franz Marc. Kandinsky formulated a conceptual distinction between what he called "the great realism" and "the great abstraction." "These two poles open up two paths, which lead ultimately to the same goal," he declared. "The great realism is a desire to exclude from the picture the externally artistic [element] and to embody the content of the work of art by means of the simple ('inartistic') rendering of the simple, hard object....The great abstraction provides the great contrast to this realism, consisting as it does of the apparent wish to exclude completely the objective (real) element and to embody the content of the work of art in 'nonmaterial' forms."[46]

Kandinsky recognized his own path as that of "the great abstraction," and he admitted to Schoenberg that he was having a little trouble locating an example of "the great realism." "I await its appearance with impatience," he wrote. "I believe it will come tomorrow."[47] In this regard, Schoenberg's paintings, and also those of the French naive artist Henri Rousseau were the answer to Kandinsky's prayers. Examples of both were triumphantly published in the *Blaue Reiter* Almanac. The freshness of the self-taught painter's vision, in Kandinsky's view, was the theoretical counterpart to abstraction and also the

Figure 38. Arnold Schoenberg: *Blue Gaze.* **Oil on cardboard. 7 7/8″ x 9″. (Schoenberg 125). Collection Lawrence and Ronald Schoenberg and Nuria Schoenberg Nono.**

antidote to academic stagnation. As he declared, the art academy "puts more or less of a brake on even the greatest and strongest talent....An academically trained man of average gifts is distinguished by the fact that he has learned to recognize the practical-purposive and has lost the ability to hear the inner sound....But if a person without artistic training—and thus without knowledge of objective, artistic facts—paints something, the result is never merely an empty sham. Here, we see an example of the effect of that inner power which is influenced only by the most general knowledge of the practical-purposive."[48] Thus Schoenberg's humble but more realistic portraits fit Kandinsky's purpose better than the "Visions." While Kandinsky identified with Schoenberg's musical compositions as an artist, he responded to the paintings as a theorist. For him, as for Loos, Schoenberg became something of a "modernist opportunity."

Schoenberg's "Visions" disturbed Kandinsky, perhaps because they broached ideas similar and yet at the same time entirely alien to his. Kandinsky detected a certain "strangeness" in these paintings, as in the work of Kokoschka, that derived from the Austrian artists' preoccupation with self. To the Germans of the *Blaue Reiter* group, this

Figure 39. Wassily
Kandinsky:
*Improvisation 28
(Second Version).*
1912. Oil on canvas.
43 7/8" x 63 7/8".
(Grohmann 1606). The
Solomon R.
Guggenheim Museum,
New York.

confessional aspect of expressionism was repugnant, and most of them found the work of both Klimt and Schiele excessively sentimental. Schoenberg's dependence on the human face as a conveyor of spiritual values irritated Kandinsky, who himself painted only one real portrait, and no self-portraits whatsoever. Kandinsky was seeking a universal spiritual abstraction beyond the self, while Schoenberg's insights remained bound up in the artist's own psyche. The painter August Macke shared his friend Kandinsky's low opinion of what he called Schoenberg's "green-eyed water-bread with its astral appearance."[49]

With Kandinsky's help, Schoenberg's career as a painter began to make some progress. No sooner had he seen photographs of the composer's paintings, than Kandinsky was making plans to include them in a Russian exhibition. While these plans never materialized, Kandinsky made sure that Schoenberg's work was shown in the first exhibition of the *Blaue Reiter* group at the end of 1911, in addition to being published in the Almanac. Schoenberg's show at Heller's in Vienna had been treated as a joke, but association with the likes of Kandinsky and Marc made him much more interesting to Austrian artists. In January 1912, Paris von Gütersloh, an original member of Schiele's *Neukunstgruppe*, invited Schoenberg to participate in a group exhibition in Budapest: "It seems to me that the picture of that which . . .we call the art of today would be only partially complete without phenomena like you and Kokoschka."[50] An entire room was given over to about two dozen of the composer's pictures. In the catalogue, Gütersloh wrote that "if Schoenberg's paintings accomplish nothing else but to make us mistrust our own judgment, . . . they have perhaps achieved their greatest secret goal. They are directed against our godless certainty and high-handedness, against our knowledge, against the fear aroused by our doubts in this [ostensibly] excellent mechanism: Man."[51] At the end of February 1912, both Gütersloh and Kandinsky contributed essays on Schoenberg's paintings to a kind of *Festschrift* put together by Alban Berg. It seemed that Schoenberg might make it as a painter after all.

However, by March 1912 it was clear that Schoenberg was having second thoughts about his second career. Kandinsky had asked him to participate in an exhibition that was being organized by the staff of the avant-garde Berlin publication *Der Sturm*. Schoenberg had personal differences with the editor, Herwarth Walden, but even putting these aside, he was not enthusiastic about the prospect of exhibiting. "I do not believe it is advantageous for me to exhibit in the company of professional painters," he told Kandinsky. "I am surely an 'outsider,' an amateur, a dilettante. Whether I should exhibit *at all* is already a question. Whether I should exhibit with a group of painters is almost *no longer a question*."[52]

Charges of dilettantism had featured prominently in the attacks on the Heller show, but it is unlikely that Schoenberg was having a delayed reaction to this criticism. Certainly he had never paid much attention to critics before, and the fact that he continued to exhibit after the Viennese showing indicates that he was not dissuaded by the negative reviews. No, this was something else. Schoenberg had come to terms with his limitations as a painter, or rather he had realized that painting was not a simple pursuit, that being a serious painter required as much effort as being a serious musician. He could not, in fact, have two careers; the time had come to make a choice, and practically speaking, there really was no choice.

Schoenberg's attempt to express himself simultaneously in several media had come to an end. Henceforth, he would continue to paint, from time to time, landscapes that pleased him, to sketch his friends and family, and, most frequently, to draw himself. These, however, were efforts totally lacking in any artistic pretensions, the work of a hobbyist or habitual doodler.[53] Whereas Schoenberg, to the end of his days, treasured the paintings from the 1908-1912 period, his two hundred-odd drawings were treated disrespectfully, stashed in stray folders or open drawers. With the completion of *Erwartung* and *Die glückliche Hand*, he came to accept that he could not singlehandedly produce a *Gesamtkunstwerk*. This had probably been apparent to him already in 1909, when he called on Pappenheim and Kokoschka for assistance. Still, he persisted in trying to fully visualize both productions, even creating detailed stage designs (Figures 40 and 41) and, for *Glückliche Hand*, costume studies. Some of these little drawings and paintings (Plates 28 and 29) are as lyrical and lovely as Schoenberg's autonomous works of art, and yet the obvious presence of footlights and the boxlike boundaries of the stage makes clear their practical function. Neither *Erwartung* nor *Glückliche Hand* are theater in the conventional sense, and each is carried primarily by the strength of its music. Just as the story lines of the two works seemed to provide a resolution to Schoenberg's personal crisis, so, too, did the attempt to master both the literary and visual aspects of a theatrical piece provide a solution to his aesthetic crisis. The subordination of art to music in the text and staging was emblematic of the place that writing and painting would thereafter occupy in his life. Though he continued to take a keen interest in staging and would occasionally write his own lyrics when compelled to by spiritual necessity and the absence of an appropriate preexisting text, this was viewed chiefly as a creative expedient. Of his various texts he later wrote, "Incompleteness . . . shows itself on the most exposed flank, and this is no doubt the reason why an artist in several art-forms has seldom had the experience of achieving more recognition than was his due from one art. On the contrary: people always conclude from that achievement which they find slight that the other one is slighter still."[54]

Schoenberg had given up painting because he realized that his efforts were inadequate and that, as a composer, he lacked the time required to perfect them. Up until now, he had been a "naive" painter, but he had never, like Henri Rousseau, been a naive man. The identity of the "naive" or self-taught artist revolves around the circumstances that separate him from the general flow of art history. Since aspiring artists normally attempt to link up with tradition by enrolling in art schools and/or studying the work of other artists, only those artists who are in some way handicapped by social, economic, or geographic factors remain remote from tradition. In the case of Schoenberg, however, none of these factors would have posed a long-term obstacle to his education as a painter, had he chosen to pursue this path. He was perfectly capable of inculcating himself in the tradition of Western picture making, just as he had in music, and he was already part of the most advanced social-aesthetic milieu in Vienna. Schoenberg could function as a naive painter only for a brief period—that is, only until he became aware of the technical and expressive limitations imposed by his lack of training.

Today, Schoenberg's "finger exercises," which Kandinsky found so appealing, are not nearly so interesting to us as the "Visions" and "Gazes." The latter evidence a curious duality, for like their creator they are at once naive and sophisticated. The artist's greatest weaknesses—his inability to formulate a complex composition, his inability to render anatomically correct proportions—here become his greatest strengths. The result, paradoxically, is a series of works that not only hold their own with those of the other expressionists, but actually transcend the very limits of expressionism by foreshadowing some of the most radical artistic developments of the century. Kandinsky, even in his abstract paintings, retained a conventional notion of composition as the arrangement of forms. Schoenberg, however, did not deal with composition, but rather with the surface of the canvas itself. In the 1960s and '70s, the color-field painters would evidence a similar preoccupation with the presence of the picture plane. However, what was to be a fairly strict

Figure 40. Arnold Schoenberg: *Glückliche Hand (setting, Scene I).* **Colored pencil on paper. 4 3/8″ x 5 1/2″. (Schoenberg 158). Collection Lawrence and Ronald Schoenberg and Nuria Schoenberg Nono.**

formal exercise for these later artists was for Schoenberg an approach fraught with expressive significance. His ability to find exact coloristic equivalents for certain emotional states, and to set these tones into effective relationships with one another, constitutes the basis for his most important achievement. To the extent that Schoenberg's visionary paintings accomplish exactly what the artist intended, and accomplish it in a manner both original and revolutionary, they may be considered great works of art. More so than the relatively traditional portraits, Schoenberg's "Visions" are proof of Kandinsky's contention that the artist unfettered by academic training is capable of instinctively making contact with the inner essence that is the ultimate creative goal.

Figure 41. Arnold Schoenberg: *Erwartung (settings)*. Crayon, pastel, and watercolor on cream wove paper. 12 1/2″ x 10 1/4″. (Schoenberg 152). Collection Lawrence and Ronald Schoenberg and Nuria Schoenberg Nono.

Figure 42. Egon Schiele: *Portrait of Arnold Schoenberg.* **1917. Black crayon and tempera on paper. 18″ x 11 1/2″. Whereabouts unknown.**

AFTERMATH

Schoenberg's brief career as a painter coincided with a period of transition and consolidation in his professional and personal life. The reconciliation with Mathilde may have been less than ideal, but Arnold found solace and, eventually, spiritual regeneration in his art. His wife resumed her role as companion and friend, someone whom he could count on to sympathize with his problems and to supervise his correspondence. A similarly uneasy equilibrium was established in Schoenberg's professional life, with continuing hardship and misunderstanding balanced by expanding recognition of his contributions as a composer and teacher.

The financial position of the Schoenberg family remained tenuous; it seemed that every small gain was compensated for by an equivalent loss, so that in the end they were no better (and possibly worse) off than they had been before. In 1910, Schoenberg moved his family from their old apartment on the Liechtensteinstrasse, which undoubtedly held more than its share of unpleasant memories, into larger quarters in Hietzing, one of the more pleasant rural districts of Vienna.[1] The added expenses of the new apartment were scarcely met by the meager returns from a 1909 contract (Schoenberg's first steady publishing arrangement) with Universal Edition. To make matters worse, the number of his students had fallen off, his daughter Trudi had reached school age, and Mathilde's health was deteriorating. These were the circumstances that prompted him to think seriously about painting as a secondary source of income and finally, to his profound chagrin, to petition Mahler for assistance. Mahler responded by immediately sending him the equivalent of one year's rent.

At the suggestion of Emil Hertzka at Universal Edition, Schoenberg began working on a book, *Harmonielehre* (Theory of Harmony), in order to more firmly establish his reputation as a teacher. As a complement to this endeavor, he managed to obtain the position of private lecturer under the auspices of the Vienna Music Academy. Rightly fearing that a full professorship was out of the question—the very suggestion provoked an anti-Semitic outburst in the parliament—he had set his sights on this more modest goal. He even offered to teach for nothing (an insane proposition, considering his financial situation), but fortunately the Academy decided to grant him a modest stipend.

The year 1911 brought many significant changes to Schoenberg's life. In February, Webern got married, and in early May, Berg followed suit. Two of Schoenberg's first and most important pupils were now fully grown. Meanwhile, in New York, Mahler had been

Figure 43. *Gertrud, Arnold, and Georg Schoenberg.* **Ca. 1912. The Arnold Schoenberg Institute, University of Southern California, Los Angeles.**

diagnosed as suffering from a then incurable streptococcal infection. Honoring her husband's wish that he be allowed to die in Vienna, Alma made arrangements for their return. In accordance with the doctor's request, few people came to see the great composer's stretcher taken off the train in Vienna's *Westbahnhof* and whisked away to the Löw sanatorium. The scene was an eerie pendant to that of Mahler's grand departure four years earlier. He died at the sanatorium on May 18. The funeral was attended by, among others, Klimt, Loos, Kraus, Altenberg, and, of course, the entire Schoenberg circle.[2] Deeply moved, Schoenberg painted a picture of the interment and subsequently dedicated *Harmonielehre* to Mahler.

Schoenberg's ties to Vienna were loosening, and in August 1911 a freak occurrence prompted him to flee. One of the tenants in his building, in a fit of madness, threatened the composer's life. Without any warning or preliminary preparations, Schoenberg suddenly turned up, alone, on the Starnbergersee in southern Germany. Berg, Webern, and some other friends quickly took up a collection so that he could send for Mathilde and the children. There, in this pleasant Bavarian summer resort, Schoenberg finally met Kandinsky face-to-face. Various forces seemed to conspire to keep him in Germany. Kandinsky's connections promised to be helpful, and a number of Berlin luminaries were launching a campaign to fund a teaching post for him. At the same time, a Viennese professorship, which he still hoped for, had not materialized.

In October 1911, Schoenberg moved into the Villa Lepke, a sort of artists' colony on the outskirts of Berlin. He arranged to teach at the Stern Conservatory and garnered the beneficent (and munificent) support of a number of wealthy patrons. Louise Wolff, director of one of Germany's leading concert agencies, decided to take him in hand. His work began to be performed throughout Europe and was published as never before. Delighted by the apparent upturn in his fortunes, Schoenberg wrote Hertzka, "You cannot imagine how famous I am here. I am almost too embarrassed to mention it. I am known to everyone. I am recognized from my photographs. People know my 'biography,' all about me, all about the 'scenes' I have occasioned, indeed, know almost more than I."[3]

Fame and fortune, however, do not necessarily go hand in hand. Trudi was suffering from open foot sores brought on by malnutrition, and Mathilde remained in poor health. Mahler, on his deathbed, had lamented, "Who'll take care of Schoenberg now?"[4] His widow, whose visits to the Schoenberg household made her guiltily aware of her superior beauty and wealth, resolved that the composer should be among the first to receive a grant from the newly founded Gustav Mahler Foundation. Webern and Berg discussed the possibilty of initiating an "Action for Schoenberg."

Berlin was hardly the paradise Schoenberg had hoped for. Like Kokoschka, who had gone there in 1910 to be nurtured by Herwarth Walden's periodical *Der Sturm* and the art dealer Bruno Cassirer, Schoenberg wanted to believe that the grass was greener on the other side of the border. He was perhaps not entirely aware that the German reaction to his music did not differ much from what he had encountered in Vienna. When his move to Berlin was announced, a local music critic suggested taking up a collection to send him back.[5] In 1912 a performance of the *First String Quartet* touched off a lengthy debate in the press. "The most daring harmony would not bother me, if it expressed anything at all," proclaimed the reviewer, Leopold Schmidt. "But until now I have never heard anything so boring and lacking in invention. One does not need to fight against this music; it will destroy itself."[6] Schoenberg was particularly peeved by the supercilious, pseudosophisticated tone of this attack. He commented in his diary, "The Viennese mob at least has a pleasing quality of laughability, which has at any rate a half-conciliatory effect. One can despise them but not hate them. But these people here, every one of whom wants to be something better, stir one up to the highest degree."[7]

On the question of which was preferable, Berlin or his hometown, Schoenberg remained ambivalent, reluctant to renounce entirely what he called "our loathed and beloved Vienna."[8] He, along with many others, recognized that "it is difficult to convince our Viennese public of the value of an artistic movement by any means other than unchallenged great success (preferably abroad)."[9] Yet he also acknowledged that Vienna, by virtue of its long and distinguished musical history, had somehow earned the right to take certain things for granted. The Germans, by comparison, were overly analytical, but not necessarily more receptive to innovation. In later years he would recall, "Berlin showed a lively and intense interest in recognizing and explaining the symptoms of a work of art, something that was missing in Vienna, thanks to centuries of experience in composing....Whatever was new was derided after several performances in Berlin, whereas in Vienna it needed only one performance. In extreme cases—in both places—no performance at all."[10]

Nevertheless, Vienna was capable of hurting Schoenberg as Berlin never could. The love he felt for the Austrian capital made that city's rejection almost impossible to forgive or forget. When, in June 1912, the long awaited Vienna professorship finally came through, Schoenberg turned it down. "For the present, I could not live in Vienna," he explained to the president of the Academy. "I have not yet got over the things done to me there, I am not yet reconciled....I know that in a very short time I should have to start fighting the very same battles I have been trying to escape from. Not because I am afraid of fighting, but because I expect the very outcome that is the end of every movement in Vienna, a draining away into shallowness."[11]

Meanwhile, the battle went on. Contrary to what Schoenberg sometimes believed, not every Viennese performance of his work provoked a scandal. Now, however, the erratic fluctuations between glory and disaster reached unprecedented extremes. After a successful performance of *Verklärte Nacht* in 1912, it almost seemed as if the tide were turning in Schoenberg's favor. "In spite of your many grievances against Vienna, even you would probably have been pleased by the pure, untarnished impression of this evening," a friend informed him. "In how short a time, actually, has the entire picture changed, if one thinks of the first performance by the Rosé Quartet...and that of today."[12] Shortly after this concert, Berg, together with Loos, Hertzka, Alma Mahler, Roller and some others, organized a drive to fund a performance of Schoenberg's monumental song cycle, the *Gurrelieder*, which had been largely written by 1901 but only completed toward the end of 1911. The concert, which took place on February 23, 1913, was a major triumph. True, as if from habit, some insisted on hissing and whistling, but for the most part the audience was jubilant—"minute-long, quarter-hour-long ovations," raved one reviewer.[13] For the first time in his career, the composer was crowned with a laurel wreath.

This success was sweet but short-lived. It was followed, scarcely a month later, by an event that many have recorded as the most scandalous in the scandal-wrought history of modern music. Pieces like *Verklärte Nacht* and the *Gurrelieder* were acceptable to the Viennese public because they encompassed one of the earliest and most traditional phases of Schoenberg's oeuvre. On March 31, 1913, a concert took place that presented not only Schoenberg's more recent *Chamber Symphony*, but also pieces by Mahler, Zemlinsky, Webern, and Berg. Now the press had a "Chamber of Horrors Symphony" to complement Kokoschka's "Chamber of Horrors" at the 1908 *Kunstschau*. In the end, however, it was not so much Schoenberg's contribution as that of Berg which occasioned the uproar.

Of all Schoenberg's comrades, Berg was the most active member of the group that clustered around Kraus, Loos, and Altenberg. The latter was an inveterate collector of postcards (Figure 45), which he used to paper the walls of his room at the Graben Hotel, mounted in albums, or, last but not least, sent to his friends. Altenberg expressed his

Figure 44. *Peter Altenberg and Adolf Loos*. Photo-postcard. Inscribed by Peter Altenberg: "Two who overcame what was previously wrong."

Figure 45. *Unidentified child*. 1917. Photo-postcard. Inscribed by Peter Altenberg: "My highest ideal." 5 1/2" x 3 3/4".

responses to the postcards—which were for the most part conventional landscape views, "cheesecake" photographs of young girls, or depictions of celebrities—by embellishing them with aphoristic inscriptions, which some considered poetry of the profoundest sort. Berg, who like Webern and Schoenberg had discovered that the relinquishing of conventional harmonic structure facilitated, and to a certain extent demanded, the creation of extremely short pieces, felt that Altenberg's brief postcard texts were ideally suited to "atonal" composition. The words and pictures had a combined effect—anticipating the conceptual art of the late 1960s and early '70s—that was somehow greater than the sum of the parts. Add music and you had a *Gesamtkunstwerk* of a highly peculiar order.

The audience on the evening of March 31 grumbled and moaned through the first numbers on the program. During Webern's piece, the hissers competed for the upper hand against those who were applauding. When Schoenberg's symphony was performed, the door keys came out. But when Berg's *Altenberglieder* were sung, the conflict between the enthusiasts and the revilers came to physical blows. During the melee that ensued, four people—a philosophy student, a doctor, an engineer, and a lawyer—had to be removed by the police.[14] Schoenberg returned to Berlin with all his worst opinions about Vienna confirmed. On the train he said, "I wish I'd had a revolver."[15]

The abrasive side of Arnold Schoenberg—the aspect that prompted the conductor Otto Klemperer to describe him as "a very angry man,"[16]—was largely a defense developed in response to a hostile public. Over the course of many painful years, youthful arrogance had been transformed into a sometimes impermeable veneer of toughness. Paranoia—or what the writer Franz Werfel, who married Alma Mahler in 1929, called "narrow-chested energy with fearful side glances"[17]—began to seem justifiable, even necessary. Schoenberg's break with tonality had constituted such a radical departure from tradition that even some of his former supporters abandoned him. Strauss brutally rejected his one-time protégé's later innovations. "The only person who can help poor Schoenberg now is a psychiatrist," he wrote Alma Mahler. "I think he'd do better to shovel snow instead of scribbling on music-paper."[18] Yet at the same time, alienation of the majority brought Schoenberg's loyal friends that much closer together. As Schoenberg himself acknowledged in his first letter to Kandinsky, "For the present there is no question of my works winning over the masses. All the more surely do they win the hearts of individuals—those really worthwhile individuals who alone matter to me."[19] Experience had taught him to view the world in terms of "us" and "them."

In 1914, when war broke out, Schoenberg was nearly forty years old. The pattern of his life and personality had been established by the events that had taken place in the waning years of Habsburg power, and these formulative experiences constituted the basis for many of his later reactions. His peculiar psychic makeup, which remained intact through his final years in America, is perhaps better documented than that of other Austrian artists of the period, many of whom died young or without leaving much concrete evidence of their opinions. Though one would hesitate to call Schoenberg typical, the various manifestations of his character can nonetheless be used as a mirror to view some of the salient traits of the era that shaped him.

The war brought Schoenberg back once again to Vienna. He was vacationing in the German resort of Murnau with Kandinsky when the Archduke Franz Ferdinand was assassinated at Sarajevo. The painter returned to Russia, his homeland, and the composer, expecting to be called up by the military, returned to Austria in September 1915. Without his knowledge, various friends lobbied to have him exempted from service, appealing now to the Austrian authorities, now to the Hungarians, under whose jurisdiction Schoenberg technically fell due to his father's place of birth. Military service aggravated a hereditary asthmatic condition, and in June 1916, the composer was sent home. Toward the end of that year, the Emperor Franz Josef, whose much-vaunted reign had lasted since 1848, died. The Empire limped on through the remaining years of the war, but it was clear that it would not survive.

One of the most prevalent misconceptions regarding "*fin de siècle* Vienna" is that radical politics were necessarily allied with radical artistic developments, and that the dissolution of the Habsburg monarchy, which subsequently came to be acknowledged (in books such as Robert Musil's *The Man without Qualities*) as historically inevitable, was necessarily perceived as such by artists while it was in fact taking place. Arnold Schoenberg, for one, wanted to believe, and actually did believe for the first years of the war, that Austria-Hungary would win. He accepted his duty as a soldier willingly, as did Kokoschka, who volunteered for combat shortly after the fighting broke out. Not only did Kokoschka volunteer (an action that caused him some embarrassment later, when he became an ardent pacifist), but he also saw to it, with the help of Adolf Loos, that he was assigned to the most prestigious cavalry regiment, the one comprising only the highest nobility. Schiele believed that the aristocracy should be reestablished,[20] and after the war Schoenberg became a confirmed monarchist, a position he never altogether renounced even after he came to accept that it was completely unrealistic. The fact that these artists all created works that challenged the existing aesthetic order to such an extent that they could be seen as political threats (for example, the Archduke Franz Ferdinand once expressed a desire to break every bone in Kokoschka's body), does not mean that any of them were politically motivated. Schoenberg firmly believed that art and politics should not mix: "It's really too stupid of grown-up men, musicians, artists, who honestly ought to have something better to do to go in for theories about reforming the world, especially when one can see from history where it all leads."[21]

There is a tendency to misconstrue the fight that Schiele, Kokoschka, Schoenberg, and many of their contemporaries waged on behalf of individual expressive freedom as a fight for democratic freedom. In fact, Vienna's cultural institutions had usually perished from a surfeit of democracy. The *Klimtgruppe*, like the Secession before it, had been established in order to protect the rights of a minority from the diluting effects of majority rule. Schoenberg had a characteristically blunt solution to such organizational disputes: dissolve the offending institution and reformulate it without the offending members. He was categorically opposed to democracy. "I believe in the rights of the smallest minority," he explained. "Democracy often acts in a manner resembling dangerously something like a 'dictatorship of the (very often extremely small) majority.'"[22]

Schoenberg's ideal political system was one in which people of genius would be, if not actively encouraged, at least left in peace: "Let every individual try to be as decent as he is gifted, as modest as he is efficient, and as inconspicuous as he is ungifted. For nothing can be done....unless there is a sufficiently large number of people with ideas and a still larger number who have been brought up not to stand in their way."[23] Possibly he was a monarchist because, in a vague, apolitical way, he equated genius with nobility. "Someone who believes in himself and respects himself is the one and only person capable of respecting and honoring merit," he wrote. "For this reason, I ... find association with the aristocracy very pleasant."[24]

Schoenberg identified democracy—the rule of the masses—with those masses who had hissed and whistled at his concerts. His disdain for his audience was immense. And yet he continued to nurture a belief, perhaps held over from his days as leader of the workers' chorus, that "it is the amateur, and it has always been the amateur, who has really promoted and encouraged art."[25] He fervently believed that music should be accessible to all who were interested. Later, in America, he would bemoan the fact that the cost of sheet music and concert tickets made such items available only to the well-to-do.

"From each according to his means" was Schoenberg's guiding principle; music was not a luxury, but a necessity, and the ideal music school or society was one that reserved a place for those too poor to afford the customary fee. This ad-hoc form of socialism may seem puzzling in view of Schoenberg's professed belief in monarchistic rule; however, it is just such a transition from monarchistic paternalism to socialistic paternalism that has characterized Austrian government in the twentieth century.

By 1917, Austrians realized that they had reached the beginning of the end, and those artists who could do so began to make plans for the postwar era. Perhaps, despite the disillusionment and pain of the war (from which Schoenberg suffered profoundly), it would become possible to realize certain prewar ideals. Early in 1917, Egon Schiele gathered together all the artists he could find in Vienna—a motley crew including Schoenberg, Altenberg, Klimt, and Hoffmann—in support of a new venture which he called a *Kunsthalle* (art hall). It was to be, he said, "not an association, but only a work group."[26] A principal aim of the project was to provide needy artists with funding derived largely from the sale of members' work and the translation of foreign poetry. As a model of cultural socialism, in which some members would donate their more marketable efforts for the benefit of their less fortunate colleagues, this plan was probably quite consistent with Schoenberg's own beliefs, although it is hard to imagine that it could ever have worked. At any rate, after securing the thirty to forty thousand kronen required to cover the first half year's operating expenses, and selecting a building site near the *Stadtpark* (city park), Schiele was apparently forced to abandon the endeavor.

Despite their mutual contact with Max Oppenheimer and Paris von Gütersloh, it is unlikely that Schiele and Schoenberg knew each other prior to this. Before the war they had rarely been in Vienna at the same time. In 1917, however, although Schiele was still serving in the army and Schoenberg had been called up again for emergency duty, both men were allowed to live at home in the city. From their acquaintance at this time stems a series of tempera and crayon portraits of Schoenberg (Figure 42), which the painter probably executed on his own initiative, as the composer could hardly have afforded to commission him. Toward the end of the year, one of the watercolors was reproduced on a postcard by the bookseller and publisher Richard Lanyi. Nevertheless, it seems that Schiele was still working on the portrait, perhaps with the intention of doing an oil (though none is known to exist or even have been started), for he used the Lanyi postcard to remind Schoenberg that he was still wanted for sittings.[27]

The end came in 1918. Austria's economic, political, and artistic life received blows from which, to some extent, the nation never recovered. In January, Gustav Klimt suffered a stroke, and after lingering for a few weeks in the hospital, he died of the resulting complications. Kokoschka had suffered a near fatal war injury and was recuperating in Dresden. In Vienna, food and fuel shortages became endemic; what little was available in the way of such amenities was quickly snapped up by the rich at exorbitant prices. Schoenberg, who had been permanently excused from military service at the end of 1917, decided to move his family to the suburb of Mödling, where living expenses were less inflated. Though naturally he continued to visit Vienna, he never again lived there. By leaving the city when he did, he escaped not only the worst deprivations of the war, but also the worst of the ravaging international flu epidemic, which spread more rapidly in an urban environment. In October 1918, Schiele's pregnant wife succumbed to the disease, and the artist himself died three days later. Armistice was declared on November 3, 1918, and on November 16, in a bloodless "revolution," six centuries of Habsburg rule came to an end.

Though in the final months of the war cultural events were difficult to arrange, Schoenberg gradually began to implement some of his ideas for reforming Austria's musical practices. When the *Kunsthalle* fell through, he considered founding some sort of artists' colony together with Webern and Berg. Mödling was less than ideal for this purpose because of its distance from Vienna, but even before public transportation was restored, Schoenberg had gathered an eager band of pupils willing to make the sixteen-mile round-trip on foot. He commuted twice a week to the Schwarzwald School, where, in accordance with his principles, he received students on a "pay as you can" basis. In June 1918 the multifaceted Heller bookshop presented a series of public rehearsals of Schoenberg's *Chamber Symphony*. The idea was that by participating in this process and studying copies of the score (which were to be sold at half price), the public would more actively enter into the ultimate realization of the musical piece. This concept found its fullest expression in the "Society for Private Musical Performances," which the Schoenberg group formally established in November 1918.

The rules of the "Society for Private Musical Performances" were designed to conform to Schoenberg's idea of a musical utopia as conceived after many years of unsatisfactory contact with the real world. As a matter of policy, performances were repeated several times, for Schoenberg, remembering that his own compositions were received favorably only upon their second or third presentation, had come to believe that repetition was necessary to instill in the public an understanding of modern music. The performances were open to subscribers only, and no applause or demonstrations of any kind were allowed. Those who could not afford the full price of a subscription were permitted to pay as much, or as little, as they wished. Critics, however, were refused admission. Unfortunately, this attempt to preselect an audience that would be favorable to modern music backfired. The Society garnered only three hundred subscribers,[28] and in the postwar period of ever-spiraling inflation, this was simply not enough. The Society was forced to suspend its activities in 1921.

"The Society for Private Musical Performances" was more than an idiosyncratic experiment; it was Schoenberg's gift to the Austrian nation. The urge to rebuild Austria's cultural life had become common among artists who, like Schoenberg, had previously felt compelled to abandon their native land for Germany. Though Schiele toyed with the idea of emigrating after the war, he nonetheless conceived of the *Kunsthalle* as a means "to stop the flight of talent from our land and to ensure that all native Austrians have the opportunity to create for the honor of Austria."[29] Schoenberg would never quite get over his feelings of ambivalence toward Vienna, but when it came to music, he was intensely nationalistic. He was appalled that one of the by-products of the war had been

Figure 46. *Gertrud Schoenberg.* Ca. 1925. The Arnold Schoenberg Institute, University of Southern California, Los Angeles.

the elimination of Austrian and German music from the international repertoire, and whenever possible, he tried to convince his colleagues in other countries to rectify the resulting inequity. This, to some extent, was also the purpose of the "Society for Private Musical Performances." "Our Society," he believed, "if it is granted just two or three years of efficacy, will educate a public whose understanding of modern music will be unlike that of any other public in the entire world. With such a public, Austria's supremacy in the field of modern music will be assured for decades to come."[30] When, in the early 1920s, Schoenberg succeeded in formulating a new system, based on twelve tones, to replace the structure that had been lost with the abandonment of conventional tonality, his thoughts again turned to Austria's position in world musical history. This invention would surely guarantee his nation's preeminence, would "show the world that *music*, if nothing else, would not have advanced if it had not been for the Austrians, and that *we* know what the next step must be."[31]

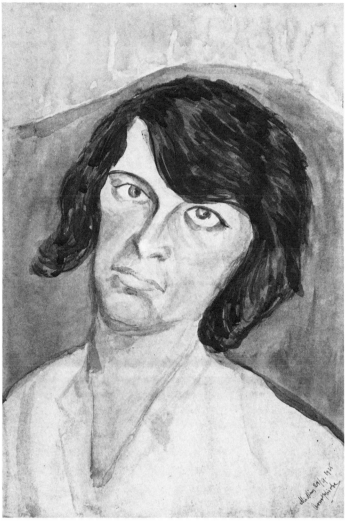

Gradually, Austria recovered from the war. The mechanisms of culture began to function again, fueled by a false optimism born of inflationary excess. Although Schoenberg's concerts still provoked occasional squabbles, his compositions were more favorably received than ever before. In 1920 the *Gurrelieder* were the hit of the Vienna Music Festival. The only major disturbance in his life came in 1923, when Mathilde, who had been ailing for years, died. On what terms they parted, one may never, and perhaps should never, know. Schoenberg himself was in Berlin at the actual moment of his wife's death and, upon learning of it, immediately painted a haunting "Vision" that bears an uncanny resemblance to her deathbed photograph.[32] Afterward, he gave her the mourning that he felt was her due. Then, almost exactly a year later, he married Gertrud Kolisch (Figures 46, 47, and 48), the sister of one of his pupils, Rudolf Kolisch.

As the war faded into the past, Schoenberg once again gathered around him his

Figure 47. Arnold Schoenberg: *Portrait of Gertrud Schoenberg.* **Pencil on ivory wove paper. 11 1/8″ x 8 3/4″. (Schoenberg 74). Collection Lawrence and Ronald Schoenberg and Nuria Schoenberg Nono.**

Figure 48. Arnold Schoenberg: *Portrait of Gertrud Schoenberg.* **1925. Watercolor. 16 1/4″ x 11 1/4″. (Schoenberg 68). Collection Lawrence and Ronald Schoenberg and Nuria Schoenberg Nono.**

customary group of loyal friends and students. Loos was back in Vienna, and the two old chums often went drinking together in the city. In the autumn of 1924, Kokoschka returned from Dresden to prepare an exhibition at Vienna's Neue Galerie, an enterprise newly founded with the mission of continuing the prewar tradition of such pioneering galleries as Miethke. Kokoschka, like many old friends, came to call at Schoenberg's house in Mödling, and stayed to paint the composer's portrait (Figure 49). One may infer that the sitter was not entirely pleased with the result, for he refused to permit the portrait to be reproduced in his fiftieth birthday *Festschrift*.[33]

Memories of the "bad old days" were provoked when, shortly after the Neue Galerie exhibition opened, one of Kokoschka's paintings was slashed. Loos insisted that his friend make the most of the publicity value of this incident; Kokoschka would have to issue a statement to the press declaring that he could not live in such a town, and then leave Vienna. With much prodding (the reluctant artist actually had to be watched to make sure he would carry out the plan), Kokoschka was finally loaded onto a Paris-bound train.[34] Thus began what he called "the time of my great journeys,"[35] during which he created numerous beautiful landscapes (Plate 19) of places such as Paris, Marseille, Madrid, Toledo, Lisbon, London, Amsterdam, Venice, Istanbul and Jerusalem. It was indicative of the postwar climate that scandal had actually become a mark of distinction. This, no doubt, is the reason why Kokoschka, in his autobiography, exaggerated the impact of the first performance of *Mörder, Hoffnung der Frauen*, turning what was actually an indifferent response into a full-scale riot.[36] Had such a riot in fact taken place in 1909, it would have been emotionally devastating; after World War I, the story was proof positive of the play's artistic merit.

Throughout Europe modernist innovations were being welcomed with open arms. If enthusiasm for this development was not altogether universal, it was nonetheless fairly clear that modernism, in all its myriad manifestations, was here to stay. "The explosive period seems to be more or less over," Kandinsky had declared already in 1914.

> On the scene of life, the great sieve appears, and what is small and trivial falls through. All the more, people will try to gobble up what is left in the sieve....The catchwords have become generally known; they can be bought for a few pennies in the newspaper....The coinage becomes smaller and greasy from many fingers....Art is made into a menagerie: the fine specimens sit in cages and a daring animal trainer with a whip in hand explains the characteristics of the artists.[37]

The "Savages" had been tamed.

Schoenberg could not help but be pleased that the scandals were diminishing in both frequency and intensity. However, he viewed the concomitant proliferation of a new atonal "school" as a violation of everything he stood for. "Damn it all!" he exclaimed. "I did my composing without any 'isms' in mind. What has it got to do with me?"[38] "This human tendency toward the fossilizing of form is shocking, even tragic," Kandinsky concurred. "Yesterday the man who exhibited a new form was ruined. Today, this same form is immovable law for all time."[39] Schoenberg himself had predicted in 1912 that "the second half of this century will spoil by overestimation whatever the first half's underestimation has left unspoilt."[40] Now he was living to see his prophecy being fulfilled thirty years before the anticipated time!

Figure 49. Oskar Kokoschka: *Portrait of Arnold Schoenberg.* **1924. Oil on canvas. 37 3/4″ x 29 1/8″. (Wingler 171). Private collection.**

The artists who created the "new" art in the first two decades of the twentieth century were not concerned with establishing a permanent style, nor did they believe that the essential nature of art should be, or even could be, altered. The slogan over the Secession doorway, "To the age its art, to art its freedom," was a renunciation of the tyranny of style—the style of the present as much as the style of the past. As Kandinsky saw it, "art . . . . is never new, but . . . must only enter into a new phase."[41] Schiele, in formulating the precepts of his *Neukunstgruppe*, made a point of explaining that, actually, there *was* no new art, only new artists.[42] On another occasion he wrote, "There is no modern art. There is just one art, and it is eternal."[43] Loos believed that architectural design, insofar as it reflected the purpose at hand, should be styleless, and he opposed the Bauhaus's attempt to indoctrinate its students in the tenets of modernism. Schoenberg grumbled:

> People have . . . a fixed concept of *modernity*, of a fashionable modernity which completely forgets personality and only grants validity to *stylish technique* . . . . Style is only important when everything else is present! And even then, it is still not important, since we do not like Beethoven because of his style, which was new at the time, but because of his content, which is always new.[44]

This "new" art, which seemed to break all the previously accepted rules, had in truth evolved organically from the traditions that it superseded and was, as such, entirely dependent on those traditions. "It is seldom realized," Schoenberg wrote, "that the hand that dares to renounce so much of the achievements of our forefathers has to be exercised thoroughly in the techniques that are to be replaced by the new methods. It is seldom realized that there is a link between the technique of forerunners and that of an innovator and that no new technique in the arts is created that has not had its roots in the past."[45] As a teacher, Schoenberg gave his students an extremely thorough grounding in the classical techniques. He did not teach *atonal* or *twelve-tone* composition; he taught *composition*; "with the emphasis on composing."

Schoenberg's theories of education were very similar to those of Kandinsky, who stated, "I do not believe that the teacher is obliged to burden . . . his student with 'immutable' laws. Rather his task is to open before his students' eyes the doors of the great arsenal of resources, i.e., means of expression."[46] Schoenberg, essentially self taught, was categorically opposed to rote learning. The gravest flaw in the existing educational system was "the way the young are stuffed with 'ready-made' knowledge and acquire only 'tangible' qualifications."[47] "I believe that art is born of 'I must,' not of 'I can,'" he stated.[48] Schoenberg was interested in "encouraging young people to look at things for themselves, to observe, compare, define, describe, weigh, test, draw conclusions and use them."[49] His goal, in short, was to teach his students to develop their talents in the way most suited to them.

When Schoenberg left Berlin in 1903, he told Strauss, "I will not forget [your help] for the whole of my life and will always be thankful to you for it."[50] Years passed, and Schoenberg and Strauss did not remain friends, but in a sense the younger composer kept his promise to this man whom he had once addressed as "honored master." In all his decades as a teacher, in all the energy and caring which he devoted—often at the expense of his own work—to his students and colleagues, Schoenberg repaid Strauss's kindness many times over. Despite his enduring poverty, he was always willing, if necessary, to take talented students for little or no pay. Berg's first year with him, for example, was "on the house." Schoenberg supported Webern with substantial loans ("far beyond what I can afford"[51]) and, when this did not suffice, tirelessly solicited the assistance of others. He wrote innumerable recommendations for grants and spontaneous letters to potential patrons on behalf of his students and fellow composers. Not only did he endeavor to help his musical colleagues, he went out of his way to further the reputations of all artists in whom he believed. When Loos, mortally ill in a sanatorium, celebrated his sixtieth birthday in 1930, Schoenberg launched a massive letter-writing campaign to found a Loos school. He knew from sad experience that great artists are often honored only after they die, and he wanted to make sure his friends were spared this deprivation. In 1934, shortly after he himself had fled Nazi Germany, he tried desperately to find an American patron for Kokoschka, whose emotional and financial stability was gravely threatened by Hitler's cultural policies.

Schoenberg's loyalty to his friends was absolute. He intuitively recognized the power and authenticity of genius and immediately embraced those whom he admired as kindred spirits: "People of a certain standing have a sense of that standing, which teaches them who is their peer and who is not."[52] As he wrote to his colleague in Amsterdam, Willem Mengelberg:

> I have always known that a great artist, a truly great one, *must be* my friend....We are not simply artist-friends, but artist-brothers. And we are brothers not simply in art, but in all human things...for it cannot be otherwise: art is the most adequate and truthful thing that people can do; there is no mask but only the truth, and whoever is an artist-brother is a human brother, a spiritual blood relation at the same time![53]

The counterpart to Schoenberg's generosity and the spiritual kinship he felt with his colleagues was an often misunderstood demand for reciprocal loyalty. People such as himself, he acknowledged, "are driven...by the great ruthless honesty with which they treat themselves and which makes them adopt the same attitude to other people as well."[54] Perhaps recalling Gerstl's betrayal, he categorically refused to allow dissension within the ranks. Although he did not demand that his colleagues emulate him—"I have written differently from Mahler and Zemlinsky, but never felt any need to take opposition to them"[55]—he did demand respect, that precious quantity he had so willingly offered his own mentors despite their differences from him. In view of his many painful memories, he would give no quarter to those who did not like his music. "I consider such people as my enemies," he declared flatly.[56] Yet he recognized that his standards could sometimes be too harsh, and that "the better sort of people become enemies faster than friends because everything is so serious and important to them."[57]

To counter his own excesses, he tried to teach himself forgiveness. "If only we could manage to be wise enough to put people on probation instead of condemning them, if we could only give proven friends such extended credit!"[58] He had a tendency to speak first and regret it later; he could end even the most aggressive letters with a meek apology and the words, "No offense, I hope."[59] When finally he felt compelled to reject former comrades, as happened all too often, he always tried to leave a way open for their return, to build them a "bridge, at least a footbridge" over which they might cross back to his side.[60] In a certain sense he could never entirely give up a friend, for he could not imagine that such a person's positive qualities could cease to exist. The spirit of a broken alliance was nonetheless enduring.

It is significant that despite the sometimes incomprehensible demands that he made of his colleagues, Schoenberg never succumbed to the petty jealousy that was so rampant within Viennese artistic circles. Even when another composer, Josef Matthias Hauer, challenged his authorship of the twelve-tone system, he managed to swallow his pride and extend his hand in friendship. Above all, Schoenberg explained, his desire to collaborate with his competitor stemmed from "the urge to recognize achievement."[61] In contrast to this attitude, Kokoschka, for example, maligned anyone who he felt challenged his preeminence as Vienna's *Oberwildling* ("Chief Fauve").[62] Schiele was described by him as "the Viennese pornographer and imitator of Klimt and me."[63] Max Oppenheimer, once his friend, was denounced vehemently as an imitator when he succeeded in obtaining a Munich exhibition before Kokoschka. Kokoschka, in a rage, dispatched Loos to rectify the situation and, if possible, sabotage Mopp's show.[64] Schoenberg, in all innocence, suggested to Loos that Franz Marc, whom the composer had just met, might be able to arrange the Munich exhibition for Kokoschka. However, when Marc showed him Loos's letter, he was shocked: "Loos . . . is annoyed about Oppenheimer, calls him a cheat and a copier of Kokoschka and warns people about him. It is wrong to do this to Oppenheimer: he is unoriginal, but one does not have to call him a cheat for that."[65] Such tactics were totally alien to Schoenberg.

Schoenberg's aggressiveness, his perfectionism, and his sometimes erratic egotism were all developed to protect his artistic integrity from the onslaught of a hostile public, and these defenses, formed in the combative prewar era, remained in place long after that era had passed. His almost pathological hatred of critics—the subjects of some of his most biting caricatures (Figure 50) and verbal attacks—and his obsessive need for multiple rehearsals—an inadequate performance, he feared, would justify the critics—can only be understood in the light of his earlier experiences. As he aged, Schoenberg withdrew more into a world where he felt safe. He relied on the support of those friends and students whom he had come to trust, and began, consciously and unconsciously, to eliminate those things in his life that caused him grief. During the war years, he expressed perverse delight in the fact that his work could seldom be performed. "In peacetime—which means wartime for me —I am quite prepared to go back to being everyone's whipping boy . . . . But for the present—more than ever—I should like to keep out of the limelight."[66] He banished all newspaper criticism from his house, even going so far as to cancel two magazine subscriptions because their reviewers were hostile to his music. He also resigned from the Austrian Association of Teachers of Music when they began publishing a critical journal. He joked that he liked being abroad because he could not really understand what was being said to him there, and hoped that his foreign friends would never hear his music. "What will they think of me when they hear my horrible dissonances?" he worried facetiously.[67]

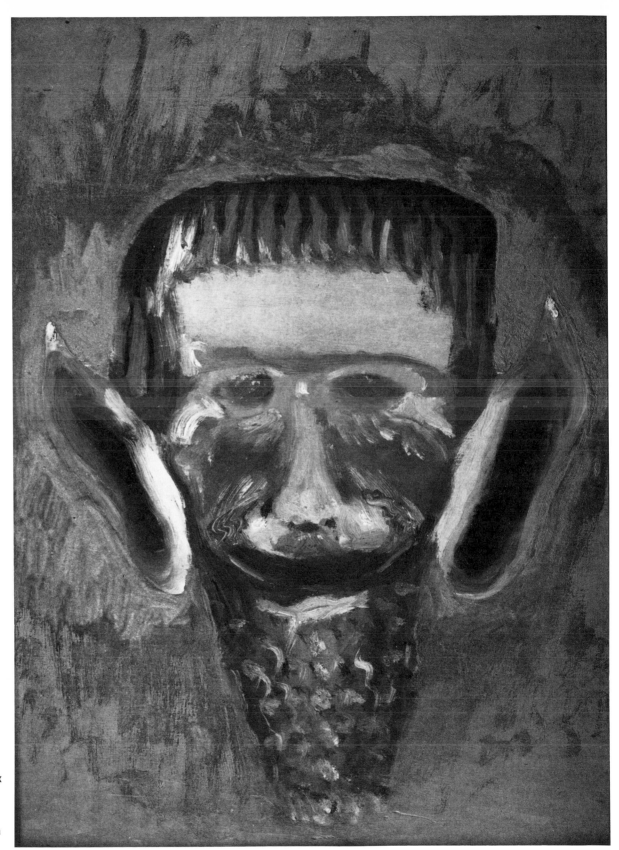

Figure 50. Arnold Schoenberg: *Critic I*. Oil on wood. 17 3/8" x 11 3/4". (Schoenberg 117). Collection Lawrence and Ronald Schoenberg and Nuria Schoenberg Nono.

choenberg had become accustomed to applying absolute moral standards to both his personal and professional life. Despite his theoretical disdain for politics, in practice he made little distinction between artistic integrity and human integrity. Thus he was among the first to perceive that the transformation of anti-Semitism from a private prejudice into a political manifesto necessitated an absolute moral choice. The specter that haunted Europe in the 1920s and '30s posed one of the greatest ethical dilemmas of the century, if not of all time. Compared to this, the malicious squabbles that had shaped Schoenberg's life before the war were nothing. Nonetheless there was a certain similarity in the tenor of the two situations: each generated its share of heroes and villains, and each left the vast majority, sheltered by cowardice or indifference, hovering on the sidelines. For that majority, the difference between passive cooperation and active collaboration was, in both instances, almost insignificant.

After the First World War, anti-Semitism infected Austria like a pernicious virus. The Salzkammergut, perhaps because of its proximity to Munich, was an early hotbed of Nazi activity. In 1921, Schoenberg was routed from his summer lodgings there by a local campaign to rid the area of all Jews. Already stung by this experience, he was deeply wounded when Alma Mahler (spurred by the same Viennese penchant for gossip that had prompted her to show the composer Strauss's insulting letter and would later cause her to instigate a notorious feud between him and the novelist Thomas Mann) informed him that his old friend Kandinsky had been bitten by the anti-Semitic bug. Kandinsky, who had returned from Russia to join the staff of the newly founded Bauhaus, wrote to Schoenberg in April 1923 suggesting that he might be able to get him a post at the *Musikhochschule* (music college) in Weimar. Schoenberg responded with an impassioned attack on anti-Semitism in general and Kandinsky in particular.

Kandinsky was a humanist who believed that intellectual values were stronger than the imperatives of race or religion. Schoenberg knew that such a stance was no longer sufficient. Kandinsky believed that he and Schoenberg, as members of the cultural elite, could stand apart from the masses. Schoenberg was content to be part of "the lump," for he realized that "on the other side . . . everything is also just one lump." "I am a Jew," he explained. "I no longer wish to be an exception."[68] Schoenberg, unlike Kandinsky, understood with frightening prescience the eventual outcome of Hitler's program:

> Have you . . . forgotten how much disaster can be evoked by a particular mode of feeling? Don't you know that in peacetime everyone was horrified by a railway accident in which four people were killed, and that during the war one could hear people talking about 100,000 dead without even trying to picture the misery, the pain, the fear and the consequences. . . . But what is anti-Semitism to lead to if not acts of violence? Is it so difficult to imagine that?[69]

Schoenberg realized that his arguments were futile; in such situations "there is no will to understand, but only one not to hear what the other says."[70] And yet, in this "new" Kandinsky, whose views seemed so alien to him, he still hoped to find, somewhere, the "old" Kandinsky who had been his ally before the war. As was his inclination whenever he quarreled with a friend, he retained his belief in the validity of the one-time friendship and thus in the possibility of a reconciliation. Kandinsky, of course, did not understand this, nor, as Schoenberg had anticipated, did he understand the composer's lengthy diatribe against anti-Semitism. Schoenberg's letter remained unanswered, and it was only by chance that the two met again, in 1927, on the Wörthersee. Schoenberg, as promised at the conclusion of his letter, addressed himself to the "old" Kandinsky, and the two parted as friends.

After turning down Kandinsky's invitation to join him in Weimar, Schoenberg eventually obtained a professorship at the Prussian Academy of Arts in Berlin. Here he stayed from 1926 until 1933, when Hitler came to power. Now there were scandals far more ominous than those that had previously interrupted his concerts. In February 1933, while Schoenberg was in Vienna giving a lecture, a student performance at the Berlin *Musikhochschule* provoked an anti-Semitic demonstration. Upon Schoenberg's return to Germany, it was announced at a meeting of the Academy senate that henceforth all Jewish influence would be eliminated from the school. Schoenberg immediately left the room, declaring that he never stayed where he was not wanted. Several weeks later, he tendered his formal resignation. Nevertheless, he lingered in Berlin, unaware of the potential danger. On May 17 he received a telegram from his brother-in-law, couched in the innocuous pleasantries that were so often used to mask serious messages in Nazi times, that warned him, "Change of climate urgently recommended."[71] Schoenberg and his family left for Paris that very day, taking with them hardly more than their toothbrushes.

Schoenberg had converted to Protestantism in 1898, but his recent experiences confirmed his identity as a Jew. In Paris he formally acknowledged these already well-established sentiments by officially reentering the Jewish faith. More than merely a return to the religion of his forebears, his reconversion was a renunciation of the policy of assimilation. Schoenberg's Jewish contemporaries had, like him, routinely sought to deny their heritage by assuming the mask of Christianity. Mahler converted to Catholicism in 1897, when he was appointed director of the Vienna Opera. Kraus, whose acerbic barbs were aimed at Jews and Gentiles alike, was baptized in 1911; Altenberg had converted in 1900. With a simple ceremony, these men tried to convince themselves that they had purchased equality, yet in the process they relinquished the spiritual support of their ancestral faith. For Schoenberg, that faith had become more important than the illusion of equality.

As early as 1912, Schoenberg began to conceive of a grandiose musical scheme that would express the incipient renewal of his religious beliefs. Possibly the traumatic Gerstl affair and the concomitant dropping away of the emotional and tonal centers of his life and music had triggered this response, which was to materialize in the never completed oratorio *Jacob's Ladder*. World War I, by undermining all Schoenberg's secular beliefs, further strengthened his religious faith. As he explained to Kandinsky,

> When one's been used, where one's own work was concerned, to clearing away all obstacles, often by means of one immense intellectual effort, and in those eight years found oneself constantly faced with new obstacles against which all thinking, all power of invention, all energy, all ideas, proved helpless, for a man for whom ideas have been everything, it means nothing less than the total collapse of things, unless he has come to find support, in ever increasing measure, in belief in something higher, beyond . . . . Religion . . . was my one and only support during those years.[72]

Now, on the eve of World War II, Schoenberg prepared to devote himself completely to the Jewish cause. "It no longer makes sense to live for art," he wrote Webern.[73] Much to Webern's dismay, he declared that "I am decided only to work in the future for the national state of Jewry....My immediate plan is to do a big tour of America, which might become a world tour, in order to raise help for the Jews in Germany."[74] Just as he had once dedicated himself to the needs of his students and colleagues, he was now ready to put his entire energies at the service of his fellow Jews. On October 25, 1933, assured of a teaching position at the Malkin Conservatory in Boston, he set sail for the United States. As it turned out, his February trip to Austria had been his last. Schoenberg would never again see his "loathed and beloved Vienna."

Schoenberg's energetic plans for the preservation of his Jewish brethren were never realized. He was not, after all, a crusader, but a composer. He found that there was very little he could do beyond writing letters, especially as he feared that any sort of public stance would bring reprisals upon those of his family and friends who were still subject to Nazi rule. Instead he endeavored to establish himself, once more, as a teacher. During his first winter in the United States, he commuted regularly between the Malkin Conservatory in Boston and New York, where he had a group of private students who met in his studio at the Ansonia Hotel. While still in Berlin, his asthma had worsened, necessitating long retreats to warmer countries such as Spain. Now chronic bronchitis forced him to look for an alternative to the harsh northeastern climate. In the autumn of 1934 he moved to Los Angeles with his wife and their two-year-old daughter, Nuria. During the course of the next seven years, Gertrud would give birth to two sons, Rudolf Ronald (born in 1937) and Lawrence Adam (born in 1941).

After a lifetime of struggle, Schoenberg found America deceptively friendly. His arrival had sparked a publicity blitz that lasted for months. He was feted with celebratory receptions and concerts, and, despite his still rocky English, was frequently prevailed upon to lecture. Without further ado he was proclaimed "the greatest of contemporary German composers."[75] He discovered, much to his surprise, that "everyone is delighted with me."[76] Where formerly he expected antagonism and dissension, here everything was easy, as balmy as the California weather, which he described as, "Switzerland, the Riviera, the Vienna Woods, the desert, the Salzburg region, Spain, Italy — all together in one place."[77] As he advised his son-in-law, the important thing was to keep smiling, always smiling. When, on occasion, things did not work smoothly, his Austrian mentality was quick to suspect duplicity. It was difficult to accept that in America incompetence was merely incompetence, not conspiratorial malevolence.

Much to his dismay, Schoenberg eventually realized that the counterpart to American amiability was ignorance and superficiality. During the academic year 1935-36 he lectured at the University of Southern California, and in 1936 he obtained a professorship at the University of California at Los Angeles. Attendance at the U.S.C. lectures was poor, especially in light of the onslaught of preliminary publicity he had received. Those who did come were woefully underqualified. "My students are so inadequately prepared,"

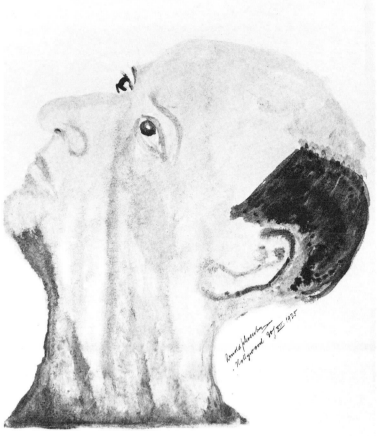

Figure 51. *Arnold Schoenberg*. **Ca. 1940. The Arnold Schoenberg Institute, University of Southern California, Los Angeles.**

Figure 52. Arnold Schoenberg: *Self-Portrait*. **1935. Brush and ink on cream wove paper. 11 1/2″ x 9 1/8″. (Schoenberg 15). Collection Lawrence and Ronald Schoenberg and Nuria Schoenberg Nono.**

he complained, "that my work is as much a waste of time as if Einstein were having to teach mathematics at a secondary school."[78] For the first time in years, he found himself reduced to teaching beginners. Child prodigies, jazz musicians, and movie composers all sought consultations with the master. As he discovered, the public's enthusiasm for his reputation did not derive from any real understanding of his work. In fact, his compositions were almost totally unknown in America. He was, understandably, furious: "These people who have been suppressing my works in this part of the world for the last twenty-five years now want to use me as a decoration...because I simply happen...to be here."[79]

Schoenberg the socialist-monarchist had entered the great capitalist morass. He had once said that he hoped his music would become the folk songs of future generations. Now he encountered a world in which the most successful composers, including many of his European colleagues, were the creators of film scores and pop tunes. This was hardly what he had had in mind. In this world, concerts were merely social events, and opera tickets status symbols purchased almost exclusively by the well-to-do. Advertising copy reduced the most profound human experiences to banal slogans. And music, under these circumstances, became just one more market to conquer.

American students, Schoenberg noted, "are extremely good at getting hold of principles, but then want to apply them too much 'on principle.'"[80] Though similar to the rote learning against which he had fought in Germany, these American practices went much further in their attempt to enshrine theoretical precepts. Theory, American musicians seemed to believe, could guarantee the future; applied methodically in assembly-line fashion, it could be used to dominate a war-weakened Europe. Schoenberg found himself inadvertently abetting a situation similar to the one he had so vehemently denounced following World War I. He was educating a generation of composers whose apparent goal was to eclipse his native tradition rather than to continue it.

His confrontation with American culture awakened in Schoenberg a nostalgia for old Vienna. Although he became an American citizen in 1941, he never truly identified with his adopted land. Forced to retire from U.C.L.A. at age seventy, he considered emigrating to a less expensive country. New Zealand appealed to him; his wife had relatives there, and he had always liked the stamps. After the war, the mayor of Vienna personally invited him to return, but his failing health and prior commitments made this impossible. Still, time had softened his former feelings of bitterness; he would have liked to have accepted the mayor's invitation. He would have liked to have helped, as he had after the first war, to rebuild Austria's cultural life. On his seventy-fifth birthday, in 1949, he was made an honorary citizen of the City of Vienna. With gratitude he acknowledged this gesture, calling it "a bond bringing me closer again to the place, its natural scenery and its essential character, where that music was created which I have always so much loved and which it was my greatest ambition to continue according to the measure of my talents."[81] Ultimately, Schoenberg could not separate the music of Vienna from the city itself. Both constituted his heritage, the root of all he had achieved.

In a perverse way, Schoenberg was grateful to Vienna for the ordeal of his earlier years. Struggle was certainly preferable to the sybaritic ease of American life. The Austrians had opposed his compositions because music mattered to them; in America, nothing mattered—the sense of urgency was lacking. Schoenberg came to believe that conflict had actually been a necessary stimulus to his work. "I had the feeling as if I had fallen into an ocean of boiling water," he recalled, "and, not knowing how to swim or get out in another manner, I tried with my legs and arms as best I could. I did not know what saved me; why I was not drowned or cooked alive....I have perhaps only one merit: I never gave up. But how could I give up in the middle of an ocean?" For this reason, he decided, "The credit must be given to my opponents. They were the ones who really helped me."[82]

Honored, in the end, both in Austria and the United States, Schoenberg's compositions never provided him with a more substantial reward: income enough to support himself and his family. After his retirement from U.C.L.A., the composer pleaded for a Guggenheim Fellowship (as he had so often done on behalf of colleagues) so that he could devote his remaining years to his own music. He was turned down. After a near fatal heart attack in 1946, perilous health became a permanent factor to contend with. Schoenberg died in July 1951, at the age of seventy-six.

It is often said that Arnold Schoenberg was a difficult man, as though being difficult were an aberration that must simply be excused because of his greatness, and not, in fact, a character trait stemming from and therefore inseparable from that greatness. Perhaps the saddest result of this is that many fail to see that Schoenberg, in addition to being a great man, was also a supremely good man who would have gone to the ends of the earth to help a friend. Sad, too, is the fact that we have come to accept compromise, the ability to "get along," as a substitute for true generosity, which derives from the adherence to a larger truth. Schoenberg was, above all, a man of principles who believed in applying absolute standards of integrity to himself and his acquaintances. The circumstances of his life—the times in which he lived and the attitudes of his contemporaries—turned him into a fighter. And that, also, is as sad as it was inevitable.

The great paradox of *fin de siècle* Vienna was that it simultaneously helped and hindered the production of culture with an intensity that has seldom been equalled. This was no hothouse (to use one observer's term), but rather a pressure cooker. The Austrians can, in this regard, be said to represent the best and worst of humankind. For every man who gave a helping hand to his colleague in time of need, there was one who tried to eradicate his colleague's achievements. For every one who told the truth, there were a dozen who lied. For every one who suffered to preserve his principles, there were a hundred who compromised and did nothing. This was true during that heady *fin de siècle* period, and it was also, unfortunately, true when Hitler marched into Austria in 1938. Culture, like politics, has its heroes and its cowards. And if, in Schoenberg's day, there were more cowards than heroes—as, indeed, there always are—it is the heroes whom we remember today, long after the cowards have perished. "There are heroes," wrote Schoenberg, "and there are composers. Heroes can be composers, and vice versa, but you cannot require it."[83] Schoenberg himself, however, was both.

NOTES

The following books have been used as principal sources and will not be cited unless specific passages are quoted:

Hahl-Koch, Jelena, ed. *Arnold Schoenberg and Wassily Kandinsky, Letters, Pictures and Documents*. London/ Boston: Faber and Faber, 1984.

Kallir, Otto. "Richard Gerstl (1883-1908) – Beiträge zur Dokumentation seines Lebens und Werkes," *Mitteilungen der Österreichischen Galerie*, XVIII:64 (1974).

Monson, Karen. *Alma Mahler, Muse to Genius*. Boston: Houghton Mifflin Co., 1983.

Neighbour, Oliver. "Arnold Schoenberg," *The New Grove, Second Viennese School*. New York/London: W. W. Norton & Company, 1983.

Rosen, Charles. *Arnold Schoenberg*. Princeton: Princeton University Press, 1975.

Stein, Erwin, ed. *Arnold Schoenberg, Letters*. New York: St. Martin's Press, 1964.

Stuckenschmidt, H. H. *Schoenberg, His Life, World and Work*. New York: Schirmer Books, 1977.

"Schoenberg as Artist," *Journal of the Arnold Schoenberg Institute*, II:3 (June 1978).

The following catalogues raisonnés have been cited in the illustration captions:

Grohmann, Will. *Wassily Kandinsky, Life and Work*. New York: Harry N. Abrams, Inc., 1958.

Kallir, Otto. "Richard Gerstl (1883-1908) – Beiträge zur Dokumentation seines Lebens und Werkes," *Mitteilungen der Österreichischen Galerie*, XVIII:64 (1974).

——. *Egon Schiele: Oeuvre Catalogue of the Paintings*. New York/Vienna: Crown Publishers/Paul Zsolnay Verlag, 1966.

Novotny, Fritz, and Johannes Dobai. *Gustav Klimt*. Salzburg: Verlag Galerie Welz, 1967.

"Schoenberg as Artist," *Journal of the Arnold Schoenberg Institute*, II:3 (June 1978).

Wingler, Hans Maria. *Oskar Kokoschka, Das Werk des Malers*. Salzburg: Verlag Galerie Welz, 1956.

Wingler, Hans Maria, and Friedrich Welz. *Kokoschka, Das druckgraphische Werk*. Salzburg: Verlag Galerie Welz, 1975.

INTRODUCTION

1. Alan Janik and Stephen Toulmin, *Wittgenstein's Vienna* (New York: Simon and Schuster, 1973).

PRELUDE

1. Throughout this book, the English spelling, "Schoenberg," which the composer adopted after emigrating to the United States, has been used in preference to the original German spelling, "Schönberg."
2. Frederic V. Grunfeld, *Prophets without Honor, A Background to Freud, Kafka, Einstein and Their World* (New York: Holt, Rinehart and Winston, 1979), p. 155.
3. H. H. Stuckenschmidt, *Schoenberg, His Life, World and Work* (New York: Schirmer Books, 1977), p. 31.
4. Karl Kraus also vied for the distinction of having been the first to "discover" Peter Altenberg. Altenberg

himself, however, gave the credit to Schnitzler.
5. Stuckenschmidt, *Schoenberg*, p. 102.
6. Ibid., p. 107.
7. Ibid., pp. 72-73.
8. Charles Rosen, *Arnold Schoenberg* (Princeton: Princeton University Press, 1975), p. 4.
9. Ibid., p. 3.
10. Sigrid Wiesmann, ed., *Gustav Mahler in Vienna* (New York: Rizzoli International Publications, 1976), p. 124.
11. The Secession was, in fact, preceded by the more informal *Siebener-Klub* (Club of Seven), whose members, including Hoffmann and Moser, met regularly at the Café Sperl.
12. Burkhardt Rukschcio and Roland Schachel, *Adolf Loos, Leben und Werk* (Salzburg: Residenz Verlag, 1982), pp. 101-102.
13. Ibid., p. 102. Loos kept his financial support of Schoenberg secret until 1928, by which time it was difficult for him to remember exactly which concert he had underwritten. Loos's contention that it was the first cannot be given much credence, as it is unlikely that the two men knew each other in 1897.
14. Claire Loos, *Adolf Loos Privat* (Vienna: Verlag der Johannes-Presse, 1936), p. 21. Loos himself ascribed this incident to the 1913 performance of the *Gurrelieder*, but Rukschcio and Schachel (*Adolf Loos*, pp. 181-182) have associated it with the more controversial group recital of the same year.
15. Rukschcio and Schachel, *Adolf Loos*, pp. 37-38
16. Alois Gerstl, "Biographische Aufzeichnungen über Richard Gerstl," in Otto Kallir, "Richard Gerstl (1883-1908) – Beiträge zur Dokumentation seines Lebens und Werkes," *Mitteilungen der Österreichischen Galerie*, XVIII:64 (1974), p. 138. Richard Gerstl's brother here lists Schoenberg, Zemlinsky, Webern, and Berg among Richard's intimates, and Mahler and Altenberg among his acquaintances.
17. Arnold Schoenberg, "Painting Influences," in "Schoenberg as Artist," *Journal of the Arnold Schoenberg Institute*, II:3 (June 1978), p. 239.
18. *Richard Gerstl (1883-1908)* (Vienna: Museum der Stadt Wien, 1983), p. 19
19. According to Victor Hammer, Gerstl's studio was located at Liechtensteinstrasse 20 (Kallir, "Richard Gerstl," p. 144), while the Schoenbergs lived at Number 68/70. Nevertheless, Hammer concurs with Dr. Egon Wellesz, who told H. H. Stuckenschmidt that the painter and the composer had shared the same building (H. H. Stuckenschmidt, letter to Otto Kallir, October 28, 1975; Galerie St. Etienne, New York).
20. Kallir, "Richard Gerstl," p. 139.
21. Gerstl studied with Griepenkerl from 1898 until the summer of 1901, at which time he dropped out to pursue his art more or less independently. He resumed his lessons at the Academy in the autumn of 1904 and stayed there for two more semesters.
22. Grunfeld, *Prophets*, p. 150.
23. Stuckenschmidt, *Schoenberg*, p. 105.
24. Kallir, "Richard Gerstl," p. 140.
25. "Testamentsentwurf," (n.d. – presumably late summer or early fall, 1908), Arnold Schoenberg Institute, University of Southern California, Los Angeles.
26. According to Dr. Egon Wellesz, Schoenberg caught Gerstl kissing Mathilde in his own house. (H. H.

Stuckenschmidt, letter to Otto Kallir, October 28, 1975; Galerie St. Etienne, New York).
27. On September 9, 1944, Otto Kallir, founding director of the Galerie St. Etienne in New York, wrote Schoenberg a letter recounting how he discovered Gerstl's work in the warehouse where it had been stored after the artist's death and resurrected it at his Vienna Neue Galerie. Kallir, who was aware only that Schoenberg and Gerstl had been friends, knew nothing about the Mathilde affair, which had been completely hushed up by Gerstl's family. "Talent is fate," Schoenberg wrote bitterly in the margin of the letter. "Very talented – to remind me of this right now." (Schoenberg Collection, Music Division, Library of Congress, Washington, D.C.)
28. Willi Reich, *Schönberg oder der konservative Revolutionär* (Vienna/ Frankfurt/Zürich: Verlag Fritz Molden, 1968), p. 53.
29. Wiesmann ed., *Gustav Mahler*, p. 42.
30. Grunfeld, *Prophets*, p. 156.
31. Rosen, *Arnold Schoenberg*, p. 6.
32. The German word "glücklich," with its combined meaning of "luck" and "fate" or "fortune," has no exact English equivalent. Carl Schorske's translation of the title as "The Golden Touch" is the most idiomatic, but it subverts Schoenberg's very deliberate symbolic use of "hands" throughout the piece.
33. Arnold Schoenberg, "Das Verhältnis zum Text," *Der Blaue Reiter*, Wassily Kandinsky and Franz Marc, eds., (Munich: R. Piper & Co. Verlag, 1912), p. 32.

34. The earliest evidence of the relationship between Schoenberg and Kokoschka is a postcard from Max Oppenheimer, postmarked September 9, 1909, addressed to the composer in Steinachkirchen: "Kokoschka was in Munich for some time. On his return, I told him about your plans and ideas, and about [your] letter. He was pleased and promised to write you. Your card shows me that he did not do this. I have not seen him in weeks, and therefore think that he is not in Vienna. As soon as I can get hold of him, I will arrange whatever is necessary..." (Schoenberg Collection, Music Division, Library of Congress, Washington, D.C.)

35. Two postcards from Kokoschka to Schoenberg would appear to date from the autumn of 1909. The first, postmarked October 13, was addressed to his Liechtensteinstrasse apartment: "Write me when I should meet you. Then I will bring with me all the preliminary notes. Always write me how much you have already written." The second card is undated: "Aren't you also starting the theater piece on Monday. The man must be halfway between softness and brutality. Do you know by heart the inner, incessant, unstoppable screams, and shattering, and mysterious ascents, and slight physical structural changes..." (Schoenberg Collection, Music Division, Library of Congress, Washington, D.C.)

36. Ibid.
37. John Russell, "Schoenberg the Painter," *Keynote*, VI:11 (January 1983), p. 12.
38. Arnold Schoenberg, "Die glückliche Hand", *Arnold Schoenberg and Wassily Kandinsky, Letters, Pictures, and Documents*, ed. Jelena Hahl-Koch (London/Boston: Faber & Faber, 1984), p. 92.

The Paintings

1. Peter Vergo, *Art in Vienna 1898-1918* (London: Phaidon Press Ltd., 1975), p. 54. Vergo points out that Hans Canon's mural for Vienna's Naturhistorisches Museum evidences a similar use of intertwined nudes.

2. Christian M. Nebehay, *Gustav Klimt Dokumentation* (Vienna: Verlag der Galerie Christian M. Nebehay, 1969) p. 212.

3. Vergo, *Art in Vienna*, p. 58

4. Ibid., p. 57.

5. Carl E. Schorske, *Fin de Siècle Vienna, Politics and Culture* (New York: Alfred A. Knopf, 1980), p. 339.

6. Burkhardt Rukschcio and Roland Schachel, *Adolf Loos, Leben und Werk* (Salzburg: Residenz Verlag, 1982), p. 108.

7. Vergo, *Art in Vienna*, p. 180.

8. Rukschcio and Schachel, *Adolf Loos*, p. 118.

9. Ludwig Goldscheider, *Kokoschka* (London: Phaidon Press Ltd., 1963), p. 9. *Die Träumenden Knaben* was published prior to the 1908 *Kunstschau*, at which Kokoschka met Klimt for the first and only time.

10. *Richard Gerstl (1883-1908)* (Vienna: Museum der Stadt Wien, 1983), p. 19.

11. Werner J. Schweiger, *Der junge Kokoschka, Leben und Werk 1904-1914* (Vienna/Munich: Edition Christian Brandstätter, 1983), p. 116.

12. Rukschcio and Schachel, *Adolf Loos*, p. 365.

13. Alois Gerstl brought his brother's work to the attention of Otto Kallir, who mounted the first Gerstl exhibition at his Neue Galerie in Vienna in 1931.

14. Robert Waissenberger, "Der Bereich der Malerei in Arnold Schönberg's Leben," *Arnold Schönberg, Gedenkausstellung, 1974* (Vienna: Universal Edition, 1974), p. 100. Waissenberger points out that a 1905 hand-painted postcard in the *Wiener Stadtbibliothek* is similar to one of Schoenberg's later cartoons, suggesting that this type of doodling occupied him from an early date. Waissenberger also dates Schoenberg's *Portrait of Hugo Botstiber* as 1906, making it one of the only paintings that can actually be attributed to the period of his friendship with Gerstl.

15. Arnold Schoenberg, letter to Emil Hertzka, March 7, 1910, in *Arnold Schoenberg, Letters*, ed. Stein (New York: St. Martin's Press, 1964), p. 25.

16. It is also possible that Schoenberg had a standing commitment from The Heller Bookshop, for in his June 16, 1910, letter to Carl Moll (see below) he referred to this as a fall-back possibility. Obviously, he would have preferred the more prestigious venue of Miethke.

17. Schweiger, *Der junge Kokoschka*, p. 214.

18. The exhibition checklist itemizes eleven portraits, two self-portrait drawings, fourteen "Impressions and Fantasies," two caricatures, five portraits of Mahler (only one of which, Figure 5, is known to survive), three "Nightpieces" (including one self-portrait), and five studies for *Die glückliche Hand*. Numbers 12 and 13 are mysteriously missing from the list, so the final count of forty-four is misleading; apparently only forty-two pieces were shown.

19. Schweiger, *Der junge Kokoschka*, p. 215.

20. Eberhard Freitag, "German Expressionism and Schoenberg's Self-Portraits," in "Schoenberg as Artist," *Journal of the Arnold Schoenberg Institute*, II:3 (June 1978), p. 164 (hereafter cited as *Journal*).

21. Arnold Schoenberg, letter to Emil Hertzka, March 7, 1910, in *Schoenberg, Letters*, ed. Stein, pp. 25-26.

22. Schweiger, *Der junge Kokoschka*, pp. 143-144.

23. Arnold Schoenberg, letters to Otto Kallir, June 5, 1945, and April 22, 1947. (Galerie St. Etienne, New York.)

24. Arnold Schoenberg, letter to Ludwig Grote, June 10, 1949, in *Schoenberg, Letters*, ed. Stein, p. 273.

25. Halsey Stevens, "A Conversation with Schoenberg about Painting," in *Journal*, p. 179.

26. Arnold Schoenberg, letter to Carl Moll, June 16, 1910. Published with the permission of The Trustees of the J. Pierpont Morgan Library, New York.

27. Stevens, *Journal*, p. 179.

28. Arnold Schoenberg, "Painting Influences," in *Journal*, p. 238.

29. Arnold Schoenberg, letter to Otto Kallir, June 5, 1945. (Galerie St. Etienne, New York.)

30. According to Jerry McBride at the Arnold Schoenberg Institute, Schoenberg owned (at the time of his death) catalogues of: the 1908 *Kunstschau*, a 1908 Goya exhibition at the Galerie Miethke, a 1910 Manet/Monet show, a 1911 *Hagenbund* exhibition, a 1912 Parisian show including work by Delaunay and Laurencin, two *Der Sturm* exhibitions (1911 and 1912), as well as most of the shows including his own work (the first *Blaue Reiter* show, the 1912 Budapest show, and later exhibitions).

31. Although Alessandra Comini ("Through a Viennese Looking-Glass Darkly: Images of Arnold Schönberg and his Circle," *Arts Magazine* 58:9 [May 1984], p. 110) suggests a 1907-08 date for Schoenberg's *Jugendstil* playing cards, Leonard Stein at the Arnold Schoenberg Institute points out that the composer signed them using the "oe" spelling of his name, something he only did after emigrating to the United States. However, it is certainly possible that the cards were signed years after they were actually created.

32. Oskar Kokoschka, letter to J. P. Hodin, October 19, 1964, in J.P. Hodin, "Kokoschka und Schiele, Eine Streitfrage," *Alte und Moderne Kunst*, XXIX:192-193 (1984), p. 46.

33. Schoenberg, *Journal*, p. 238.

34. Ibid.

35. Ibid., p. 237.

36. Arnold Schoenberg, letter to Wassily Kandinsky, December 14, 1911, in *Arnold Schoenberg and Wassily Kandinsky, Letters, Pictures and Documents*, ed. Jelena Hahl-Koch (London/Boston: Faber and Faber, 1984), p. 40.

37. Arnold Schoenberg, "Das Verhältnis zum Text," *Der Blaue Reiter*, Wassily Kandinsky and Franz Marc, eds., (Munich: R. Piper & Co. Verlag, 1912), p. 33.

38. Arnold Schoenberg, letter to Wassily Kandinsky, January 24, 1911, in *Schoenberg and Kandinsky*, ed. Hahl-Koch, pp. 23-24.

39. Schoenberg, *Journal*, p. 237.

40. Vergo, *Art in Vienna*, p. 195.

41. Ibid., p. 193.

42. Even at their most abstract, Kandinsky's forms still had underlying representational import; however, by 1913 these references had become purely symbolic.

43. Wassily Kandinsky, letter to Arnold Schoenberg, Jaunuary 18, 1911, in *Schoenberg and Kandinsky*, ed. Hahl-Koch, p. 21.

44. Ibid.

45. Wassily Kandinsky, "The Paintings of Arnold Schoenberg," in *Schoenberg and Kandinsky*, ed. Hahl-Koch, pp. 182-184.

46. Kenneth C. Lindsay and Peter Vergo, eds., *Kandinsky, Complete Writings on Art, Volume One (1901-1921)* (Boston: G. K. Hall & Co., 1982), pp.242-244.

47. Wassily Kandinsky, letter to Arnold Schoenberg, February 6, 1911, in *Schoenberg and Kandinsky*, ed. Hahl-Koch, p. 27.

48. Lindsay and Vergo, *Kandinsky, Complete Writings*, pp. 251-252.

49. H. H. Stuckenschmidt, *Schoenberg, His Life, World and Work* (New York: Schirmer Books, 1977), p. 142.

50. Schweiger, *Der junge Kokoschka*, p. 216.

51. Ibid., p. 217.

52. Arnold Schoenberg, letter to Wassily Kandinsky, March 8, 1912, in *Schoenberg and Kandinsky*, ed. Hahl-Koch, p. 48.

53. Schoenberg's technical facility and aesthetic sense continued to play a role throughout his life. He enjoyed puttering around in his workshop, making useful objects (mostly inventions, such as tape dispensers and skirt hangers, that had not yet been invented, or musical "toys," such as a cardboard violin or a twelve-tone sliderule). He made much of his own furniture and decorated the family's humble apartment in the Villa Lepke in Berlin. Later, he lamented that he could not afford to live in one of Loos's houses and looked for someone to design a reasonable facsimile.

54. Arnold Schoenberg, "Foreword to the Texts," in *Schoenberg and Kandisnky*, ed. Hahl-Koch, p. 89.

Aftermath

1. Both Klimt and Schiele had their last studios in Hietzing. The Schoenbergs' apartment, coincidentally, was next door to that of Schiele's future in-laws, the Harms family, and across the street from the building where Schiele himself would later live.

2. Burkhardt Rukschcio and Roland Schachel, *Adolf Loos, Leben und Werk*, (Salzburg: Residenz Verlag, 1982), p. 159.

3. Arnold Schoenberg, letter to Emil Hertzka, October 31, 1911, in *Arnold Schoenberg, Letters*, ed. Erwin Stein (New York: St. Martin's Press, 1964), p. 31.

4. Sigrid Wiesmann, ed. *Gustav Mahler in Vienna* (New York: Rizzoli International Publications, 1976), p. 113.

5. Frederic V. Grunfeld, *Prophets without Honor, A Background to Freud, Kafka, Einstein and Their World* (New York: Holt, Rinehart and Winston, 1977), p. 151.

6. Jelena Hahl-Koch,ed. *Arnold Schoenberg and Wassily Kandinsky, Letters, Pictures and Documents* (London/Boston: Faber and Faber, 1984), p. 193.

7. H. H. Stuckenschmidt, *Arnold Schoenberg and Wassily Kandinsky, Letters, Pictures and Documents* (London/Boston: Faber and Faber, 1984), p. 193.

8. Ibid., p. 296.

9. Arnold Schoenberg, letter to the Board of the Imperial Royal Academy of Music and the Fine Arts, Vienna, Spring, 1910, in *Schoenberg, Letters*, ed. Stein, p. 38.

10. Arnold Schoenberg, letter to The Deutsche Allgemeine Zeitung, June 18, 1930, ibid., p. 142.

11. Arnold Schoenberg, letter to Karl Wiener, June 29, 1912, Ibid., p. 32.

12. Rukschcio and Schachel, *Adolf Loos*, p. 168.

13. Ibid., p. 179.

14. Ibid., p. 182.

15. Peter Vergo, *Art in Vienna 1898-1918* (London: Phaidon Press Ltd., 1975), p. 16.

16. Stuckenschmidt, *Schoenberg*, p. 141.

17. Alma Mahler Werfel, *And The Bridge is Love, Memories of a Lifetime* (New York: Harcourt Brace & Co., 1958) p. 104.

18. Arnold Schoenberg, letter to an unknown correspondent, April 22, 1914, in *Schoenberg, Letters*, ed. Stein, p. 50.

19. Arnold Schoenberg, letter to Wassily Kandinsky, January 24, 1911, in *Schoenberg and Kandinsky*, ed. Hahl-Koch, pp. 22-23.

20. According to Schiele's nephew, Anton Peschka, Jr.

21. Arnold Schoenberg, letter to Josef Rufer, December 18, 1947, in *Schoenberg, Letters*, ed. Stein, p. 252.

22. Arnold Schoenberg, letter to William S. Schlamm, June 26, 1945, ibid., p. 234.

23. Arnold Schoenberg, letter to the Chairman and

Committee of the German Students' Commonroom, Prague, ca. February 12, 1914, in *Schoenberg, Letters,* ed.Stein, pp. 48-49.

24. Arnold Schoenberg, letter to Paul Bekker, August 1, 1924, ibid., p. 109.

25. Arnold Schoenberg, letter to Jacques Martet, January 6, 1950, ibid., p. 279.

26. Egon Schiele, letter to Anton Peschka, November 29, 1917, in Christian M. Nebehay, *Egon Schiele, Leben, Briefe, Gedichte* (Salzburg: Residenz Verlag, 1979), p. 417.

27. Egon Schiele, postcard to Arnold Schoenberg, November 29, 1917. (Schoenberg Collection, Music Division, Library of Congress, Washington, D.C.)

28. Of the three hundred subscribers, Schoenberg ruefully noted that only two hundred were "good ones." Schoenberg in *Schoenberg, Letters,* ed. Stein, p. 142.

29. Nebehay, *Schiele,* p. 417.

30. Rukschcio and Schachel, *Adolf Loos,* p. 233.

31. Arnold Schoenberg, letter to Josef Matthias Hauer, December 1, 1923, in *Schoenberg, Letters,* ed. Stein, p. 104.

32. John Russell, "Schoenberg the Painter," *Keynote,* VI:11 (January 1983), p. 13.

33. Rukschcio and Schachel, *Adolf Loos,* p. 300.

34. According to Fanny Kallir, wife of Otto Kallir (the founder of the Neue Galerie).

35. Ludwig Goldscheider, *Kokoschka* (London: Phaidon Press Ltd.), 1963), p. 16.

36. Vergo, *Art in Vienna* pp. 248-249. Vergo was the first to point out that the Viennese newspapers contain no record of any sort of "riot" at the 1909 premiere of *Mörder, Hoffnung der Frauen.* Schweiger (*Der junge Kokoschka,* pp. 110-113) quotes several reviews of the performance that suggest that bad weather turned the entire event into something of a washout.

37. Wassily Kandinsky, letter to Arnold Schoenberg, February 5, 1914, in *Schoenberg and Kandinsky,* ed. Hahl-Koch, p. 61.

38. Arnold Schoenberg, letter to Wassily Kandinsky, July 20, 1922, ibid., p. 74.

39. Wassily Kandinsky, letter to Arnold Schoenberg, February 6, 1911, ibid., p. 27.

40. Arnold Schoenberg, circular letter to his friends, September 16, 1949, in *Schoenberg, Letters,* ed. Stein, p. 290.

41. Wassily Kandinsky, letter to Arnold Schoenberg, January 26, 1911, in *Schoenberg and Kandinsky,* ed. Hahl-Koch, p. 25.

42. Nebehay, *Schiele,* p. 112.

43. Arthur Roessler, ed., *Egon Schiele, Briefe und Prosa* (Vienna: Verlag der Buchhandlung Richard Lanyi, 1921), p. 19.

44. Arnold Schoenberg, letter to Wassily Kandinsky, September 28, 1913, in *Schoenberg and Kandinsky,* ed. Hahl-Koch, p. 60.

45. Arnold Schoenberg, "A Self-Analysis," 1948, in Stuckenschmidt, *Schoenberg,* p. 548.

46. Wassily Kandinsky, "Comments on Schoenberg's Theory of Harmony," in *Schoenberg and Kandinsky,* ed. Hahl-Koch, p. 131.

47. Arnold Schoenberg, letter to Intendant Flesch, October 4, 1929, in *Schoenberg, Letters,* ed. Stein, p. 135.

48. *Schoenberg and Kandinsky,* Hahl-Koch, ed., p. 146.

49. Arnold Schoenberg, letter to Intendant Flesch, in *Schoenberg, Letters,* ed. Stein, p. 135.

50. Stuckenschmidt, *Schoenberg,* p. 66.

51. Arnold Schoenberg, letter to a Dutch patron, July 9, 1923, in *Schoenberg, Letters,* ed. Stein, p. 100.

52. Arnold Schoenberg, letter to Thomas Mann, November 1, 1930, ibid., p. 144.

53. Arnold Schoenberg, letter to Willem Mengelberg, June 1, 1920, in "Schoenberg in the Netherlands," *Journal of the Arnold Schoenberg Institute,* VI:2 (November 1982), p. 199.

54. Arnold Schoenberg, letter to Hanns Eisler, March 12, 1926, in *Schoenberg, Letters,* ed. Stein, p. 121.

55. Arnold Schoenberg, letter to Paul Stefan, April 24, 1923, ibid, p. 87.

56. Arnold Schoenberg, letter to Paul Bekker, ibid., p. 109.

57. Arnold Schoenberg, letter to Hanns Eisler, ibid., p. 121.

58. Arnold Schoenberg, letter to Paul Bekker, ibid., p. 109.

59. Arnold Schoenberg, letter to Emil Hertzka, February 6, 1913, ibid., p. 39.

60. Arnold Schoenberg, letter to Hanns Eisler, ibid., p. 121.

61. Arnold Schoenberg, letter to Josef Matthias Hauer, ibid., p. 104

62. The critic Ludwig Hevesi was responsible for this nickname.

63. Oskar Kokoschka, letter to J. P. Hodin, October 19, 1964, in J. P. Hodin, "Kokoschka und Schiele, Eine Streitfrage," *Alte und Moderne Kunst,* XXIX: 192-193 (1984), p. 46.

64. Werner J. Schweiger, *Der junge Kokoschka, Leben und Werk 1904-1914* (Vienna/Munich: Edition Christian Brandstätter, 1983), p. 203.

65. Stuckenschmidt, *Schoenberg,* p. 142.

66. Arnold Schoenberg, letter to Alexander von Zemlinsky, October 9, 1915, in *Schoenberg, Letters,* ed. Stein, pp. 52-53.

67. Charles Rosen, *Arnold Schoenberg* (Princeton: Princeton University Press, 1975), p. 37.

68. Arnold Schoenberg, letter to Wassily Kandinsky, April 19, 1923, in *Schoenberg and Kandinsky, ed. Hahl-Koch, p. 76.*

69. Arnold Schoenberg, letter to Wassily Kandinsky, May 4, 1923, ibid., pp. 80-82.

70. Ibid., p. 82.

71. Rukschcio and Schachel, *Adolf Loos,* p. 387.

72. Arnold Schoenberg, letter to Wassily Kandinsky, July 20, 1922, in *Schoenberg and Kandinsky,* ed. Hahl-Koch, p. 74.

73. Rukschcio and Schachel, *Adolf Loos,* p. 389.

74. Stuckenschmidt, *Schoenberg,* p. 270.

75. Grunfeld, *Prophets,* p. 178.

76. Arnold Schoenberg, letter to Rudolf Kolisch, August 27, 1934, in *Schoenberg, Letters,* ed. Stein, p. 188.

77. Grunfeld, *Prophets,* p. 178.

78. Ibid. It should be pointed out that Schoenberg's later classes at the University of California at Los Angeles included advanced students as well as beginners. His love of teaching was such that he eventually came to perceive this situation as a creative challenge, out of which evolved a number of significant music textbooks.

79. Arnold Schoenberg, letter to Otto Klemperer, November 8, 1934, in *Schoenberg, Letters,* ed. Stein, p. 192.

80. Arnold Schoenberg, letter to Ernst Krenek, December 1, 1939, ibid., p. 210.

81. Arnold Schoenberg, letter to the mayor of Vienna, October 5, 1949, ibid., p. 277.

82. Stuckenschmidt, *Schoenberg,* p. 546.

83. Arnold Schoenberg, letter to Kurt List, October 17, 1944, in *Schoenberg, Letters,* ed. Stein, p. 219.

Plate 3. Gustav Klimt: *The Battle of Life (The Golden Knight).* **1903. Oil, tempera, and gold leaf on canvas. 39 3/8″ x 39 3/8″. (Novotny/Dobai 132). Private collection.**

Plate 4. Gustav Klimt: *The Black Feather Hat.* **1910. Oil on canvas. 31 1/8″ x 24 3/4″. (Novotny/Dobai 168). Private collection.**

Plate 5. Richard Gerstl: *Woman with Feather Hat.* **Oil on canvas. 39″ x 31 3/8″. (Kallir 34). Private collection.**

Plate 6. Richard Gerstl: *Self-Portrait in Front of Stove.* **Oil on canvas. 27″ x 21 5/8″.** *Self-Portrait (unfinished),* **verso. (Kallir 22). Collection Viktor Fogarassy.**

Plate 7. Richard Gerstl: *Self-Portrait (unfinished).* **Oil on canvas. 27″ x 21 5/8″.** *Self-Portrait in Front of Stove,* **verso. (Kallir 22). Collection Viktor Fogarassy.**

Plate 8. Richard Gerstl:
Self-Portrait with
Palette. **Oil on canvas.**
73 1/4″ x 23 1/8″.
(Kallir 45). Historisches
Museum der Stadt
Wien.

Plate 9. Oskar Kokoschka: *Self-Portrait with Hand on Chest.* **1913. Oil on canvas. 32 1/8" x 19 1/2". (Wingler 72). The Museum of Modern Art, New York; purchase, 1941.**

Plate 10. Richard Gerstl: *Landscape.* **Oil on canvas, mounted on cardboard. 14 7/8″ x 20 1/2 ″. (Kallir 17). Private collection.**

Plate 11. Egon Schiele: *Red Earth.* **1910. Oil on canvas, mounted on wood. 20 1/2″ x 19 3/4″. (Kallir 118). Private collection.**

Plate 12. Egon Schiele: *Portrait of a Man Pulling Garment over Head.* Ca. 1910. Crayon and watercolor on brown paper. 17 1/2″ x 12 1/8″. Collection Mrs. Alice M. Kaplan.

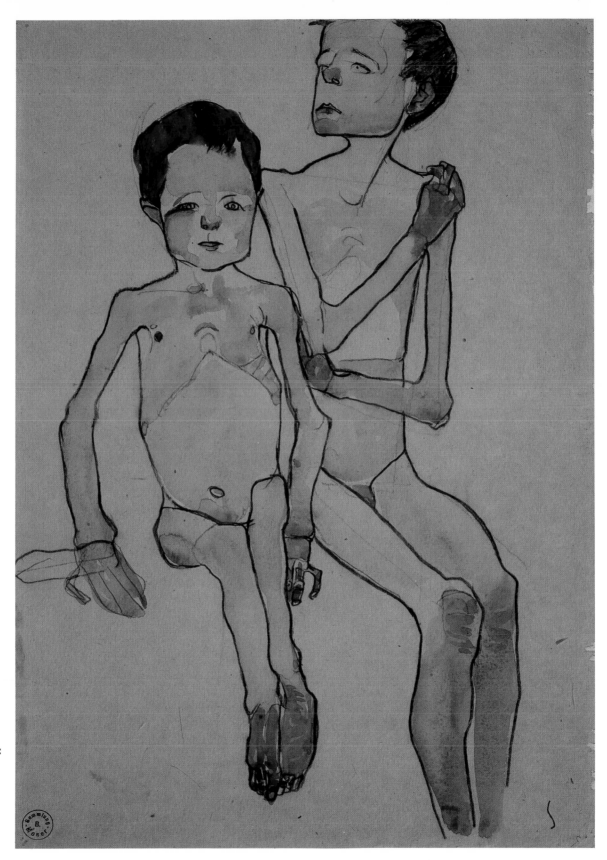

Plate 13. Egon Schiele:
Two Seated Nude
Boys. Ca. 1910.
Charcoal and
watercolor on buff
paper. 17 3/4″ x
12 1/2″. Private
collection.

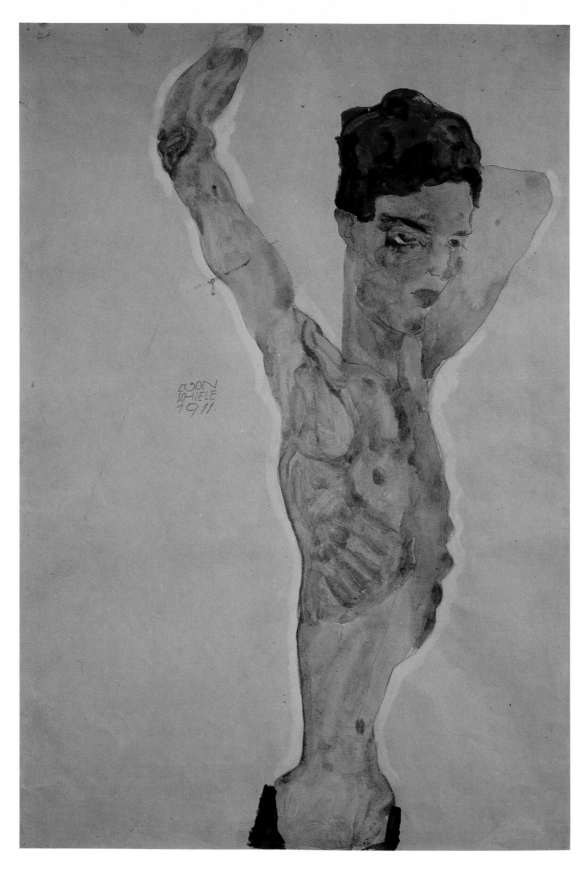

Plate 14. Egon Schiele:
Standing Male Nude.
**1911. Pencil and
gouache on ivory wove
paper. 19″ x 12 1/2″.**

Plate 15. Egon Schiele:
Sleeping Girl. **1911.**
Pencil and watercolor
on ivory wove paper.
19 1/8″ x 12 3/8″.

Plate 16. Egon Schiele:
Self-Portrait in Jerkin
with Right Elbow
Raised. **1914. Crayon,**
watercolor, and
gouache on paper.
18 3/4″ x 12 1/4″.
Collection Mrs. Alice
M. Kaplan.

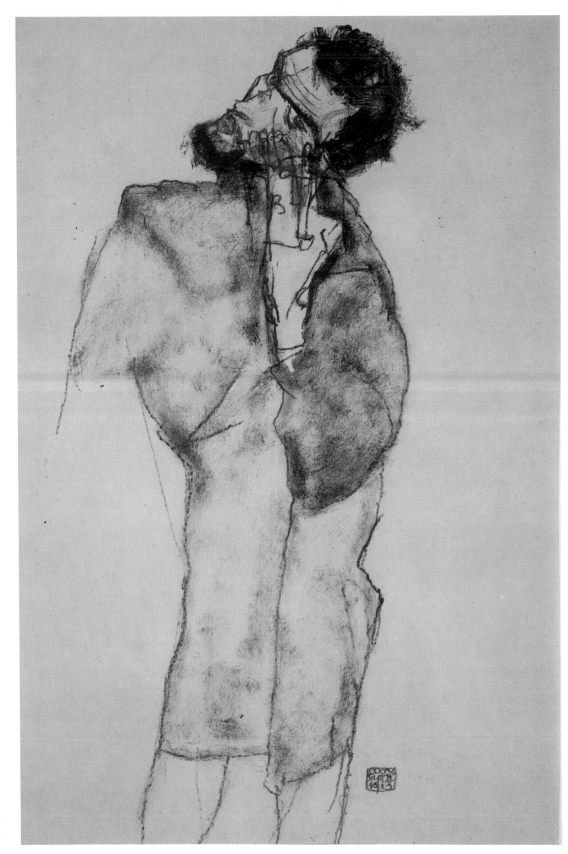

Plate 17. Egon Schiele:
Bearded Man, Standing.
**1913. Pencil and
tempera on ivory wove
paper. 18 1/4" x 12 5/8".
Private collection.**

Plate 18. Egon Schiele: *Landscape.* **1916. Pencil and tempera on yellowish wove paper. 11 5/8″ x 18 1/8″. Private collection.**

Plate 19. Oskar Kokoschka: *Courmayeur et les Dents des Géants.* **1927. Oil on canvas. 35″ x 51 1/4″. (Wingler 229). The Phillips Collection, Washington, D.C.**

Plate 20. Oskar Kokoschka: *Portrait of Felix Albrecht Harta.* 1909. Oil on canvas. 28 3/4" x 20 5/8". (Wingler 13). The Hirshhorn Museum and Sculpture Garden, Smithsonian Institution, Washington, D.C.

Plate 21. Oskar Kokoschka: *Portrait of Mrs. Karpeles.* 1912. Oil on canvas. 39 1/4" x 29 1/4". (Wingler 65). The Hirshhorn Museum and Sculpture Garden, Smithsonian Institution, Washington, D.C.

Plate 22. Arnold Schoenberg: *Portrait of Gertrud Schoenberg.* Pastel on grayish wove paper. 6 3/8" x 3 3/4". (Schoenberg 71). Collection Lawrence and Ronald Schoenberg and Nuria Schoenberg Nono.

Plate 23. Arnold Schoenberg: *Portrait.* **Oil on canvas. 26 3/4″ x 21 1/4″. (Schoenberg 85). Collection Lawrence and Ronald Schoenberg and Nuria Schoenberg Nono.**

Plate 24. Arnold Schoenberg: *Self-Portrait.* **1910. Oil on wood. 12 1/4″ x 8 5/8″. (Schoenberg 3). Collection Lawrence and Ronald Schoenberg and Nuria Schoenberg Nono.**

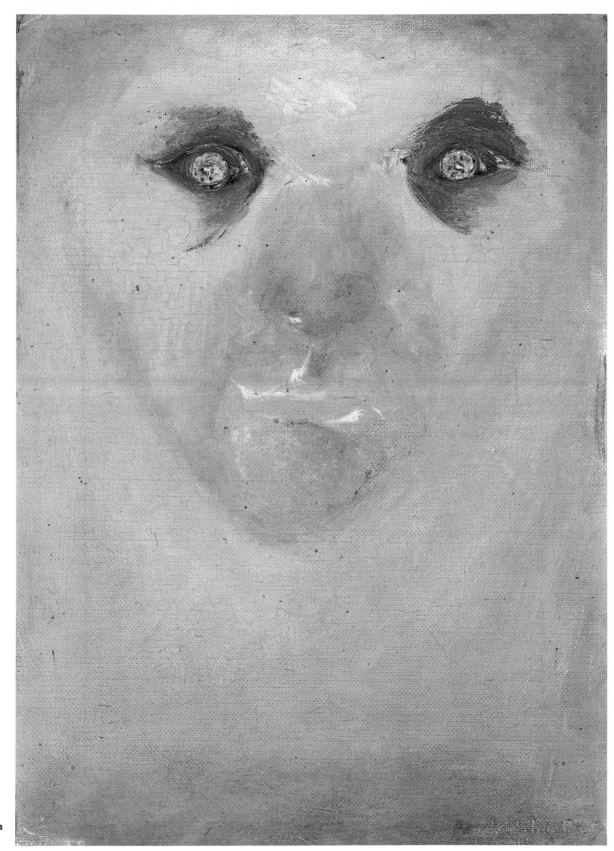

**Plate 25. Arnold
Schoenberg:** *Gaze.*
**1910. Oil on canvas.
11″ x 7 7/8″.
(Schoenberg 124).
Collection Lawrence
and Ronald
Schoenberg and Nuria
Schoenberg Nono.**

Plate 26. Arnold Schoenberg: *Landscape.* **Oil on cardboard. 14 1/2″ x 19 3/4″. (Schoenberg 146). Collection Lawrence and Ronald Schoenberg and Nuria Schoenberg Nono.**

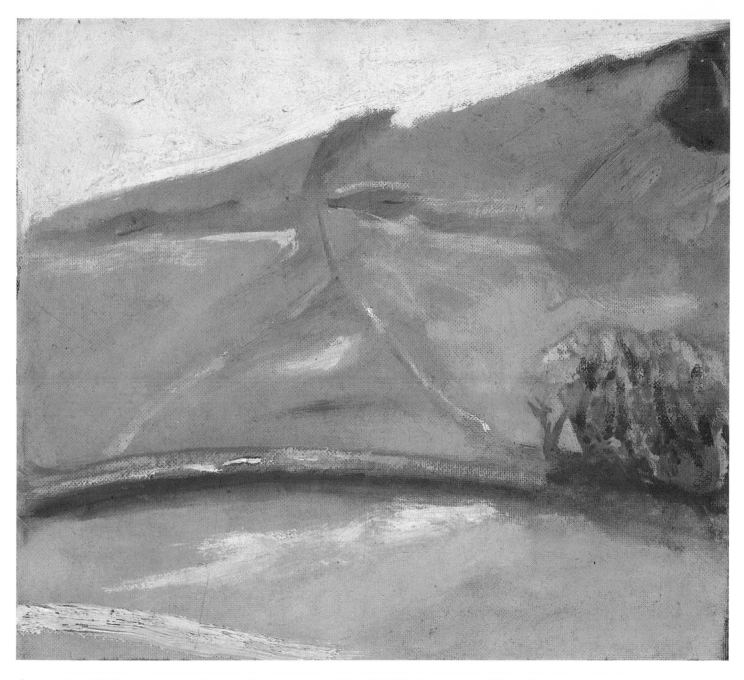

Plate 27. Arnold Schoenberg: *Landscape*. Oil on canvas. 9 1/8″ x 10 5/8″. (Schoenberg 141). Collection Lawrence and Ronald Schoenberg and Nuria Schoenberg Nono.

Plate 28. Arnold Schoenberg: *Glückliche Hand (setting, Scene II).* **Watercolor and ink wash on paper. 4″ x 5 1/2″. (Schoenberg 161). Collection Lawrence and Ronald Schoenberg and Nuria Schoenberg Nono.**

Plate 29. Arnold Schoenberg: *Glückliche Hand (setting, Scene II).* **Oil on cardboard. 8 5/8″ x 11 3/4″. (Schoenberg 162). Collection Lawrence and Ronald Schoenberg and Nuria Schoenberg Nono.**

ACKNOWLEDGMENTS

Arnold Schoenberg's paintings, largely as a result of Kandinsky's praise, have always constituted one of the most interesting unexplored facets of the history of expressionism, but they have never before been the subject of a comprehensive New York exhibition, much less a book. The idea for the present project originated with Alessandra Comini, professor of art history at Southern Methodist University in Dallas, who called my attention to the existence of the Schoenberg legacy of paintings and drawings at the University of Southern California. Because Schoenberg sold few of his works, his oeuvre remains virtually intact, and as I learned in the course of my research, one of the first to suggest a retrospective exhibition was my grandfather, the late Dr. Otto Kallir, who broached the idea to Schoenberg himself in the 1940s. Now, some forty years later, I am pleased to say that this plan is finally being carried out, and at the same time, a long-standing art-historical oversight is being corrected.

For their help in the realization of this project, thanks must go first and foremost to the composer's children, and in particular to Lawrence Schoenberg. My sincerest appreciation is also extended to Jerry McBride at the Arnold Schoenberg Institute and to Wayne Shirley at the Library of Congress in Washington, D.C.; archivists are surely the great unsung heroes of the scholarly world. Important "behind the scenes" help was provided by Franz Eder of the Verlag Galerie Welz, Olda Kokoschka, Heinz Spielmann of the Museum für Kunst und Gewerbe in Hamburg, Leonard Stein at the Arnold Schoenberg Institute, Robert Waissenberger of the Historisches Museum der Stadt Wien, and, of course, the entire staff of the Galerie St. Etienne, in particular Hildegard Bachert and Margery King. Special thanks go to the Austrian Institute in New York and Lufthansa German Airlines, whose support made possible the Austrian loans to our exhibition. Last but certainly not least, I would like to express my gratitude to all the museums and collectors whose works are reproduced herein, and to those who lent to the exhibition: the Arnold Schoenberg Institute at the University of Southern California in Los Angeles; the Solomon R. Guggenheim Museum and the Museum of Modern Art in New York; the Historisches Museum der Stadt Wien, the Österreichische Galerie and the Österreichisches Museum für Angewandte Kunst in Vienna; the Hirshhorn Museum and Sculpture Garden of the Smithsonian Institution and the Phillips Collection in Washington, D.C.; Joan Ben Avi; Viktor Fogarassy; Carolyn Hammer; the Estate of Otto Kallir; Alice M. Kaplan; Lawrence and Ronald Schoenberg and Nuria Schoenberg Nono; and a number of collectors who have asked to remain anonymous.

—Jane Kallir